A collection of stories
redefining family norms

the stigma of single
MOTHERHOOD

WRITTEN BY

Dr. Jill Zambon

Along With 11 Inspiring Authors

Cover photo credit: Caitlin Castellini Photography

ISBN: 979-8-9869367-2-7

Table of Contents

INTRODUCTION

The Parent Project was created in 2022 by Dr. Jill Zambon. After abruptly becoming a single mom just weeks before her wedding in 2014, she made the decision that just because her daughter was being raised in a one-parent household, she was not going to go without. Dr. Jill is now on a mission to help other single moms provide the same level of confidence, financial support, and opportunities to their kids as well.

The Parent Project began as an offering to other successful single moms to share their stories of motivation and strength with other single moms who have felt they could not speak out about their own stories. Quickly, it became apparent that women needed in-person collaboration and networking, and the **Transform Your Life conferences** were established in November 2022.

Still, a struggle remains for single moms that are trying to balance work and home. Dr. Jill recognized the need to help place these moms into more flexible, higher paying jobs, and in November 2022 began to stand up her staffing solutions. She now helps place single moms and military spouses into more flexible and better paying jobs.

Dr. Jill has created a Facebook group called The Parent Project Women's Group, where she shares knowledge about things like: financial management, how to get involved in our community, and upcoming conferences and book writing opportunities.

As Dr. Jill has continued to get national exposure through joining the speaking stage with individuals such as Dave Seymour, star of A&E's show Flipping Boston, and joining the DocuSeries reality TV show, The Blox, with Wes Bergmann from MTV's Real World and The Challenge – her reputation continues to shine. She continues to speak at high visibility conferences, and brings more attention to this movement.

Shattering the Stigma

Shattering the Stigma of Single Motherhood

There are an estimated 15.6 million single moms in the U.S. alone, and with divorce rates hovering between 40-50%, this number continues to grow. In the midst of their pain and fear, single moms have no choice but to grind and bear it, and make sure they are providing for their children and themselves. Oftentimes, they are shunned for being a single parent and treated like they are incomplete because there is no male counterpart in their life. They are degraded for taking child support from a father who may or may not be involved. And many have kept quiet about domestic violence situations at home.

This book is for the single mom, or the married woman who feels like a single mom, that needs encouragement and support. Whether she is already raising a child on her own, or trying to figure out if she can do it on her own, this collection of stories is a vulnerable account of women who have overcome all the obstacles and barriers that are placed in the way, and created a life that they are proud of for themselves and their children.

We believe that every woman should have the ability to share their story without shame, embarrassment, guilt, or fear of punishment.

By grabbing this book, it shows that you, too, are ready to **Shatter the Stigma.**

Shattering the Stigma of Single Motherhood is written for women looking to embrace the life of a single mom, rather than be embarrassed or feel ashamed of it. Learning how to forgive and heal from the inside out, and overcome the challenges of raising a child on their own. Each reader of this book will come away with the tools and steps they need to provide themselves and their child with the best life possible.

The Parent Project offers:

- Book co-authoring opportunities
- Transform Your Life conferences
- Staffing solutions for single moms and military spouses
- Staffing solutions for employers in IT, healthcare, pharmaceuticals, and life sciences
- Coaching for women who want to write their own books

We won't stop supporting and encouraging women to embrace their circumstances and make the most of their lives, despite the obstacles. This is just the beginning of our global movement.

When the only way to look was inward, she found the true power of her soul.

With Love,
DR. JILL ZAMBON
THE PARENT PROJECT
www.jillzambon.com

Jill Zambon

CEO & Founder of The Parent Project

https://www.linkedin.com/in/jillian-zambon-ed-d-mba-pmp-a5959725/
https://www.facebook.com/jillian.zambon/
https://www.instagram.com/jillzambon/
www.jillzambon.com

Dr. Jill Zambon is a reality TV star, single mompreneur, and real estate investor. She served 5 years in the U.S. Navy and 12 years in corporate I.T. healthcare. In 2020, Dr. Zambon founded her own business but realized she was still trading time for money. So, to spend more time with her daughter, she learned the secrets behind flipping houses and real estate income. But it wasn't always easy. After discovering infidelity, Jill split with her fiancé just two weeks before the wedding and found herself sleeping on a futon at her dad's house with her new baby. Experiences like this drove her to uncover her hidden process to gain back time and extra income – even while you sleep. She now teaches the system to single moms who want an easy way to passive income so they can free up time and ease financial worry.

IN LOVE WITH A DREAM

By Jill Zambon

In a matter of seconds, my life went from planning a wedding and a honeymoon to sleeping on a futon in the back of my dad's house with a newborn. We merely had a diaper bag for her, a duffel bag of clothes for me, and a half-used pack of diapers. None of this was part of my plan. Not the wedding, not the baby, and not the broken engagement.

The truth is, I cannot even say for sure if my relationship was *real* love, or if I was falling blindly into the *idea* of having this beautiful, perfect, little family. All I wanted was a house on a hill with a couple of kids and a husband that had a big family that spent a lot of time together—and didn't drink. And that's exactly what I *thought* I had found.

I'm embarrassed to say that I probably would have "fallen in love" and wanted to start a family with any man that came along at that point in my life. I was in my late 20s and had just returned from a few years of active duty in the Navy. I was going through a divorce when I met my daughter, Jayde's, dad. I felt like my time was running out to have a baby, get married for the long haul, and settle down.

I had always been a bit of a wild spirit—and that is probably the biggest understatement ever. I never liked to stay in one place for long. I never got too attached to people. I never felt content, and I sure as hell never planned on "settling down."

But the day I found out I was pregnant, my entire world flipped upside down and I decided it was finally time to stop the shenanigans. It was time to stop all the partying, the late nights, the one night stands, the belligerent mistakes, and the jumping around from town to town, even state to state, trying to find the one thing that would make me happy.

The day I found out I was pregnant really doesn't stand out as a memorable day. I think it was right around Thanksgiving, as we were both home from work. We may have both been home from work due to hangovers as well, I'm not sure. Regardless, it was a fluke that I even considered I might be pregnant. I was one of those girls who never had a normal period; it never came on time, and oftentimes I didn't get one at all.

This particular morning, though, some strong internal voice just said, "You need to take a pregnancy test." Because I had missed my period so many times before, and despite being on birth control from a very young age, I still kept tests around—just in case! When I got out of the shower that morning, I decided I would take one of those pregnancy tests just to make sure, especially since I was getting ready for another holiday drinking bender.

After getting out of the shower and drying myself off, I took out one of the boxes of pregnancy tests. I pulled out one of the sticks, opened the plastic wrapper very gently, and sat on the toilet holding the stick just right to let a stream of urine run across the top. I set it on the sink countertop beside me as I wiped and washed my hands. When I looked over, I saw that two blue lines had already appeared on the test.

"That can't be!" I thought to myself. "It's been, like, five seconds!" I stood in the bathroom, alone, staring at the stick and not believing my eyes. The faint blue lines turned darker and darker until I knew—it wasn't wrong.

"Well, but still… maybe that one expired," I told myself. "I should really try a different brand and see if it gets the same results." I called my partner to come into the bathroom for a second. He opened the door as I pointed to the test.

"Wait, does that mean you're…"

I stared at him, wide-eyed, and shook my head. "I think we need to go to the drugstore and get more tests though. This one might be expired," I explained.

"Okay," he replied. "Do you want me to come with you?"

"Sure!" I said. The ride to the drugstore was quiet. There were thoughts swirling in my head about how I was ever going to be a mom. I had just been married to another man for three years, and never had a child. Never even talked about having a child. Now, here I was, with this guy I had been with for four months. We had decided, together, that we would try to have a child in about a year once my body had weaned itself off of birth control. But to get pregnant in one month after being off birth control, when I had been on it for over eleven years, just didn't seem feasible.

My mind raced thinking about how much I had been drinking. I started to worry that the baby would be born with fetal alcohol syndrome. I started to worry how someone who could barely take care of herself was going to be able to take care of another human being. I started to worry about how small our house was, what if the dogs didn't like the baby, where would our kid go to school? My mind immediately went to all the "what ifs," and I wasn't even entirely sure that I was pregnant.

Well, long story short, I took about five more at-home pregnancy tests. Every single one of them came back positive. But, just to be sure, I scheduled an appointment at Planned Parenthood. It seemed like I should see if the "experts" got the same results as me, or if I had managed to pick out six dud pregnancy tests from the store.

"Welp," the nurse said, "you're definitely pregnant!" I sat in the patient exam room with her, holding a tissue, as tears rolled down my cheeks. "Are you happy or sad?" she asked.

"Happy, I think…" I giggled.

"Is that dad out there in the waiting room?" she asked.

"Yes," I replied.

"Would you like me to have him come in so I can tell him the news?"

"Sure, that'd be great," I said.

As the nurse closed the door to walk out of the patient room, I just stared at the wall in disbelief. I had never seen myself as a motherly figure. I wasn't kind. I wasn't nurturing. I didn't care about anyone else but myself. And now, I was going to have to take care of someone else!? I felt the walls of the cool room closing in around me as I stared blankly at the wall. But a funny thing happened.

Happy tears started to stream down my face. I now had a reason to take care of myself. I now had a reason to want more in life. And most importantly, I now had a reason—even a mandate—that I had to be sober for the next nine months. Sobriety was not something I had experienced for close to fifteen years, and I was a little afraid of how it would go.

But my thoughts were interrupted when the nurse walked my partner into the patient room.

"Take a seat," she said, as she motioned her hand to a chair right next to mine. He reached his warm hand over and put it over top of my hand.

"You guys are pregnant," the nurse said, flatly, unsure of what his reaction would be.

"What!?" he said, excitedly, in a high-pitched voice.

"So you're happy about this as well?" the nurse asked.

"Yes!" he said excitedly.

"Oh good," said the nurse. "Ms. Zambon is excited about it as well! The next steps will be for you guys to find a hospital or a midwife that you like and start your prenatal treatment. We have done all we can here for today. Do you have any questions?"

I laughed, thinking about the millions of questions I already had rolling around in my head. But we were so excited, neither one of us asked a single one.

When we got out to the parking lot, my partner embraced me in a huge hug and gave me a kiss on my forehead. 'You're going to be the best mom," he said.

"And you'll be the best dad," I said. And I knew he would be.

The next nine months were a whirlwind. We renovated the downstairs bedroom to be a cozy nursery, equipped with a crib, changing table, and of course a cute wall sticker tree with monkeys dangling off it. We were so ready for this baby.

The pregnancy was easy. I didn't get morning sickness,—I actually lost weight at first, and my face got thinner because I was abstaining from alcohol. I felt an inner sense of peace and calmness that I had never experienced in my life. I continued to exercise and started to try and eat more nutritional food (although Ben & Jerry's Coffee Heath Bar Crunch and Krueller twisty donuts were my go-to snacks!).

Things were going smoothly, and the topic of marriage came up frequently. We decided we would wait until after the baby came to iron out all the details, because selfishly, I didn't want to be fat in a wedding dress!

There really was no big pivotal moment in our relationship that I can remember things starting to fall apart. I don't recall us fighting, ever. My family embraced him, and I was a part of his family as well. There were small signs that came up, but when I confronted him about them they were brushed aside and I felt like I was overreacting.

Then a point came that I could no longer ignore the signs. It was a text that finally pushed me over the edge and tapped into the gut feeling that I had all along—I could not trust him. Lying had been a serious issue for the duration of the relationship, and at times had even driven a wedge between myself and people I was the closest to, including my dad.

When things finally did unravel and I decided to confront the issue head on, things came apart quickly. When I made the decision to call off the wedding, he agreed with such ease and carelessness that I knew it was over. Not just for him. My daughter and I deserved better than to be treated like this by *anyone*.

Here I was… a highly educated, brilliant, beautiful, intelligent woman. I gathered my last bit of dignity and decided I did not care if this person had fathered my child. I did not care if we were supposed to get married. I did not care what the small-town minded people were going to say about us. I knew for me, and for my baby, we weren't sticking around to wait for him to make up his mind that we were important. I already knew we were.

The first thing I needed was a place to live. Our savings were drained because we had been paying for a wedding. My credit cards were maxed out to pay for a honeymoon we never went on. And my credit was stretched, because I had bought him a truck. So my options were fairly minimal and I needed something quickly.

I turned to my dad, and asked for a place to live, which he happily obliged despite the fact that our relationship was strained and on the rocks. When I stopped sleeping at night, he recommended I go to a psychologist and get sleeping meds while he and my step-mom offered to stay up with the baby that night. They helped feed Jayde. They watched her while I got ready for work in the morning. And when I found my first house, my dad came to check it out with me and make sure it was a good home.

As I picked up the pieces of my broken life, the first thing I did was buy my own house. This was so empowering as I had always been in a relationship and never thought I'd be able to buy my own house. The house was a newer home, with a deck that overlooked the town. It had the most beautiful sunrise, and I could watch it as I sat at the kitchen table drinking my morning coffee. I had gotten a new job with much higher pay, and I had started doctorate school so I could position myself to continue to move up in my corporate career. Things were coming together, and although I still felt broken on the inside, from the outside my life looked pretty and shiny.

The problem was, I didn't know what to do with my time when I didn't have my daughter. My alcoholism snuck up on me, and before I knew it, I was actively drinking again, especially when my daughter was gone for the weekend. The more I drank, the worse the decisions I made were. I found myself in a series of bad relationships with men who were younger than me, emotionally unavailable, and although they were very attractive, the sexual chemistry was non-existent. I felt disgusting about myself and the more men I slept with, the more alcohol I drank and the more disgusting I felt. It was a horrible cycle that I felt I would never get out of.

I avoided doing any "inner work" so to speak, for well over eight years. I did everything I could to try and distract myself from dealing with how broken I was feeling. I skipped around from job to job, from place to place, trying to avoid the beliefs that were boiling over inside me. I used education and career growth as a mask.

But eventually, I couldn't run away anymore. There was no education, no career, no physical relocation that was going to heal me. It wasn't until I moved to Florida and looked for a new therapist that I learned that there are therapists that deal with people who have experienced infidelity trauma. As I started to work with her and we began to peel back the layers of the betrayal, I realized that this broken engagement was just the wakeup call I needed to heal the underlying trauma I had experienced in my life. Slowly, I started to rewrite the messages I told myself, and my beliefs. I found a career in real estate, and helping other single moms made me happier than any corporate job I had ever been in. I started to be more selective with the people I let into my life, got sober, and found a relationship with a higher power that I had never experienced before.

When I was going through the break-up and betrayal with my ex, I would have never dreamed that I would get sober, raise a child on my own, and become an entrepreneur. But as the fog lifted over my life, and as I continued with therapies such as EMDR and other trauma-focused therapies, my mind and body got healthier.

I've also come to terms that separately, he and I are both hard-working and intelligent people. Together, we did not bring out the best in each other. We did not bring out the best parents in each other, we did not bring out the best professional in each other, and we sure didn't bring out the best romantic partner in each other.

Now, I am finally able to use my story as a source of hope and inspiration for other women. If you are recently a single mom, or if you believe you may be in a relationship where you could end up a single mom, I want to invite you to check out my website at www.jillzambon.com where you can find resources and upcoming events for single moms. We would love to have you be a part of this amazing community!

Krystal Casey

CEO & Founder of The Aerial Yoga Mom
Registered Yoga Instructor

https://www.linkedin.com/in/krystalcasey/
https://www.facebook.com/flightofthephoenixcollective
https://www.instagram.com/theaerialyogamom/
www.krystalcasey.com
www.theaerialyogamom.com
https://linktr.ee/krystalcasey

A woman with a history of trauma, motherhood unlocked a portal of pain Krystal Casey didn't realize existed within. Years of traditional treatment proved unsuccessful, so she began searching for a natural alternative of healing, which led her to yoga.

Inspired by the positive changes she experienced, Krystal wanted to support women with similar struggles.

She opened a studio and spent several years learning to find balance both on and off the mat. It was a wonderfully chaotic and heady time, but overnight it all came crashing down.

Krystal was blindsided when her husband was charged with sexual abuse against a minor. Within weeks of this discovery, he overdosed.

She was devastated.

But with 5 children watching, she couldn't give up.

Instead, she returned to her practice and her tribe, and let them carry her through.

Now, she shares these experiences to help women create transformational changes in their lives.

STILL STANDING

By Krystal Casey

When I think of successful women, I'm not the first one that comes to mind. Truthfully, it wasn't that long ago that I felt like I was failing at everything: my health, my business, my marriage, and most especially my role as a mother.

You see, I grew up watching single moms do it all. My grandma, my aunts, my mom… I watched them fight, struggle, and suffer to do everything on their own, and I promised myself from a very early age that that wasn't going to be me.

Me? I was going to break *all* of the cycles. And trust me, there were a lot of them. Dropping out of school, teen pregnancy, domestic violence, addiction, divorce, sexual abuse… it was *all* going to end with me. I wasn't going to be that girl. I had seen too much, grew up too fast, knew better, and wouldn't tolerate it.

And I certainly wasn't going to let any of it happen to my children.

Turns out, I failed at pretty much all of that.

— ; —

I wed my grade school love when I was 25, and we were married for almost 12 years. In that time, we had five children and built what should have been a perfect life: we lived in a storybook kind of town where I was blessed to stay home with our kids until they started school. We made friends, enjoyed local activities, and settled into the kind of cozy that you can only find in small-town life.

During that time, I began to test the waters of entrepreneurship. This navigated me to my passion for empowering, educating, and entertaining women as a Pure Romance consultant. Eventually, I opened an aerial yoga and dance studio, building it from the ground up with dreams of leaving behind a family business as part of our legacy.

The studio was going great, but sadly, life at home was far from perfect. I wanted to believe that it could be— if only I worked a little harder, tried a little more, loved a little stronger, waited a little longer...

The hard truth is: nothing I did could have changed the outcome. But if I went back and did it again, I'd pay attention to the red flags instead of waving them away.

— ; —

Abuse colors many chapters of my life, both as a child and as a mother. The difference between then and now is I'm not staying quiet about any of it.

Not anymore.

I can clearly recall being brave enough when I was younger to disclose to a trusted family member that I was being sexually abused. She simply sighed, told me it happens sometimes and to move on; that my abuser was "still family" and essentially to pretend that it didn't happen.

I was flabbergasted. That was the last thing I expected her to say or expect me to do. I kept it quiet, but I soon moved out of the home where I was being molested.

A few months later, I realized someone had opened a cell phone account in my name without my permission and had stopped paying the bill. Turns out, it was my abuser. I filed a police report and asked a so-called friend to go with me to the interview. I had decided that I was going to come clean about everything, and I confided this information to my friend.

The morning of the interview, she backed out and I panicked about going alone; panicked at the thought of seeing him again and having to stand up to him in front of everyone in court. I panicked at the thought of being made to sound like a fool, of no one believing me and everyone learning about the awful things that had happened. So instead of driving to the police station, I sat in my car and cried.

I stayed quiet for years after that, never telling anyone about the abuse except my therapists and a few very close friends: like my husband.

You can imagine my horror and disgust then when I found out that he had repeated the horrible cycle of abuse. The same cycle he knew I was adamant about breaking. The same man who had been my strongest advocate against childhood sexual abuse for the better part of a decade.

The second I discovered the ugly truth about my husband, I removed my children without hesitation and reported him to the authorities.

In an instant, I was a single mom.

The end of our story was swift and sudden. I braced for a fight that never came. Within weeks of my discovery, he was found unconscious with a mix of meth and alcohol in his blood.

More secrets. More lies. More pain.

He left us traumatized, shattered, and confused. He left me to clean up the mess he made. He left me to figure it out on my own.

When it first happened, I broke down in front of my son. I felt like such a *failure*. I couldn't hold back the pain. "I'm so angry, and hurt, and scared," I let slip between heavy sobs.

"Scared of what?" he asked.

"Scared of doing all of this alone!"

"But Mama, why?" he asked, confused, "You've always done it alone."

Those words hit me square in the gut. *You've always done it alone.*

As soon as he said it, I could hear the echo of other voices in my life that had been telling me that all along. Here I had been fighting for my marriage for years because I didn't want to break up "the team." I kept convincing myself we were better together and thought the kids didn't see, didn't know how much I was struggling... because the whole time, I had been doing it alone.

Well, I wasn't about to stop. I had done it this long alone; I could keep going alone. I had to, for my kids.

The next year was a struggle. I went into survival mode— after all, I had five little ones to keep caring for, a funeral to plan, paperwork to complete, groceries, laundry, dishes, and trash that never stopped... The to-do list was never-ending and it was up to me to make sure it all got done.

Eventually, we fell into a "new normal" and went about our lives the best we could. We moved into a smaller, more manageable house. The kids started a new school year, and I tried to focus on my business again. But it wasn't long before I fell into a deep, dark depression.

It wasn't fair! This wasn't the plan! He promised me he'd always be here for me. We were supposed to be raising this family together— the one we *chose* to create. Why hadn't my vision been clearer? Why wasn't my intuition stronger? What had I done wrong? Was I so awful that I deserved all this pain?

I remember the morning the struggle became too much for me to bear any longer. I found myself crumpled on the kitchen floor, unable to stop crying after an especially hurtful argument with my oldest child. Exasperated, I called my sister and begged her to take my kids and drive me to the hospital. I didn't have anything left inside of me and I was ready to give up. I was convinced my children would be better off with anyone but me; I didn't want to be a mother anymore. I didn't want to do this by myself. I didn't want to live.

Fortunately, I reached out for help. My sister flew to my aid and activated my tribe for support. I checked myself into that hospital and stayed for over a week. Over the next several months I received treatment, medication, and counseling. I allowed myself time to process, to grieve, to begin to heal, one day at a time. After a while, I accepted that I could create a brand-new life for myself and my family. Soon, I began to actually believe that I could.

I started to have hope once again. I slowly rediscovered and rebuilt my confidence. I created a vision of the life I wanted and began taking tiny steps each day to make it a reality, not knowing how or if it would become true.

But it is.

This past summer, I made the cross-country move with my family that I had dreamed about! We're in a new home, making new friends, and building a new future that we're each looking forward to in our own way. The days are not always easy, and they're nearly never calm or quiet, but each one is worth it.

— ; —

When I think of successful women, I may not be the first one that comes to mind, but I know I'm on the list. I'm learning to define and enjoy my success now. I may not be where I thought I'd be at this point in my life, but I'm still standing despite every obstacle that has tried to knock me down. I am *not* a failure.

I am not a failure because I had to ask for help. I am successful because I could have chosen to end my story, but I chose not to. I am successful because I continue to care for my mental well-being with self-love. This looks different each day but includes everyday things like showering, wearing clothes I like and fit me well, styling my hair or applying makeup, eating balanced meals throughout the day, drinking water, making my bed, and tidying up around the house. For me, it also looks like taking my medication, going to therapy, yoga/meditation, journaling, and spending time doing things I enjoy. Every tiny accomplishment is a success.

I am not a failure because my marriage didn't work out the way I imagined it would. I am successful because I know I put in 100%. And because of that relationship, I've learned what I need, what I enjoy (emotionally, mentally, and physically), and who I am as a woman. I've also realized what truly matters in a relationship and what I want my children to see and develop in their own relationships as they grow.

I am not a failure because I had to close down my business and start over. I am successful because I *can* start over; because I know that I can achieve anything I put my mind to and that there is an abundance of opportunity out there waiting for me.

I am not a failure because my children have endured a childhood they need to heal from. I am not a failure because I repeated ingrained trauma and childhood patterns. I am successful because I'm breaking those patterns by breaking my silence. I am successful because I'm going to continue to use my voice and teach my children to do the same. I am successful because my children open up to me and love me and feel safe with me. I am successful because they know that I love them and am proud of them and think they are all beautiful and smart and strong and amazing!

I am successful because I grew up watching some *incredible* single moms do it all. Inspirational women who were true examples of what it means to succeed; Mothers who taught me that it takes a village to raise a child, that magic happens when you find your tribe, and that it's okay to accept help when you need it; Women who taught me to have faith in myself as a mom and that I'm stronger than I know; Single moms whose examples were encouragement that I was going to make it to the other side. Who taught me it's important to keep going, but it's also necessary to fill my own cup along the way. Who taught me the power and the beauty of leaning into womanhood.

And here I am: still standing.

Not only am I "still standing" but today I'm living the life I want, on purpose and with purpose.

That's *exactly* what success looks like.

— ; —

Now I'm on a mission to pass along these lessons, help break generational cycles, and be a source of encouragement for women everywhere. By sharing my story as an author and public speaker I get to help moms create their own villages, connect with their tribes, and watch their own magic happen. As a women's empowerment coach, I get to share the power and the beauty of leaning into womanhood and embracing our sexual selves. Through my work as a yoga instructor, I get to teach moms how to create space and time for themselves, how to nurture the mind, body, and soul, how to relax, relieve stress, and practice self-love. I also get to encourage these same women to have faith in themselves as moms and remind them that they are stronger than they will ever know.

I'm still standing, but I'm not alone anymore.

Neither are you.

If you need some support in your life, or you're a yoga lover like me, I'd love to connect. Follow my story at https://linktr.ee/krystalcasey.

Sara Schreiner

Author & Nurse

https://www.facebook.com/sara.schreiner.54
https://www.linkedin.com/in/sara-schreiner-421a7541
https://www.instagram.com/gypsara/

Sara Schreiner is a Registered Nurse with a Master's degree in Healthcare Administration. Sara has spent the majority of her twenty-year career focusing on Women's Health and more recently on Nursing Education and Professional Development. She is a Certified Bereavement Counselor for Fetal Loss and Infant Death; she has found helping and supporting families through the loss of a newborn to be the most satisfying and fulfilling part of her career. Born and raised in the Philadelphia suburbs, Sara settled on Boston's north shore and became a single mom after a long battle with infertility when she adopted two siblings at ages two and three. She is passionate about spending time with her kids and traveling. Sara has three amazing siblings and two awesome parents all in the Philadelphia area that manage to be supportive and shower her little family with love and support!

MY SAVING GRACE

By Sara Schreiner

I've always been one of those people with a plan. My plan was to marry at 24 and have kids at 26, 28, and 30. But, things never go the way we want, do they? While my life whirled into a seven year undergrad college party, I watched my friends graduate, get married, and have kids.

By 32, I found myself a successful life partner. He came with two kids, so I gave up on wanting my own. As I continued to drink, I managed to buy a home, earn a Master's Degree, and land a great job—but our relationship imploded.

After getting sober, I decided I needed a physical and mental reset. A road trip across the country was exactly what I needed to clear my mind and heal my soul. I found myself in the California desert, working in the nursery and step-down NICU unit at a hospital just miles from the Mexican border. At first, I wasn't sure what I was doing there.

Shortly after I started, I got my answer—she was born. She came into this world addicted to opiates and benzos, tested positive for marijuana, methamphetamines, and PCP. She had four other siblings scattered all over the Valley. After a few days of working in the nursery and giving this sweet baby morphine, clonidine, and phenobarb, I was in love. I decided to adopt her. I was eventually awarded temporary custody, but as quick as the biological mother decided she would go to rehab, the court took her away. I handed her over to a stranger with a sordid past and an unstable future. I still pray every night she is safe, happy, and thriving, and that the system didn't lose her. I pray her mother's love is more powerful than addiction, and that she knows love and security. I pray she knows she was wanted and someone fought for her.

After grieving and lots of self searching, I still wanted to be a mom. There was no way I could face a loss like that again. So, at 39, I decided to have my own baby, and I scheduled an appointment at a fertility clinic. The fertility specialist ran my labs and we discussed options. He said, "I'll have you pregnant by October." That was just two months away. I was elated.

I had a blast browsing online sperm bank profiles for my double helix donor. This was online dating on steroids—and there was no fear of rejection. I set out to create the most perfect human. I wanted a donor with musical ability, well educated, athletic, and with family values. I wanted tall with dark hair and light eyes. I was going to off-set every physical flaw I had and give this kid every talent I ever wanted. I created a spreadsheet with columns for IQ, education, athletic ability, career, hobbies and musical talents, and extras like languages and military service. I shared the spreadsheet with three friends and my sister and let the scoring begin. The donor with the highest score was going to be the father of my baby!

I spent $900 on donor 12064 and purchased my first vial of sperm. Thirteen million of the little guys to be exact. I had my first IUI. I slithered onto the floor and sat in that legs-up-the-wall yoga pose, said a prayer, and hobbled out of the office and back to work. I waited. I wasn't pregnant. So I bought more sperm, and did it again. And again, and again, and again— six times. Each time the devastation was worse. Each time the hatred for my body grew. I was angry. I was angry at God— this is the one thing my body was supposed to be able to do. I was supposed to be able to make a baby. We are literally delivering the sperm to the egg, what more do you want? I met with the doctor and we decided to try IVF. This was getting expensive. I did three rounds of IVF. I was almost $70,000 invested and no baby. Baffled, he re-ran all my labs. I was 41 and in early menopause; I was not getting pregnant.

I decided that night that I was done; I was not supposed to be a mom. This was obviously not what God had in store for me. My heart was hollow, my bank account was drained, my uterus was empty, and my future was bleak.

My sister, my greatest cheerleader, and the most gentle pesterer one will ever meet got it in her head that I should adopt. I was scared. I wasn't going to risk falling in love and being hurt again. But this chick wasn't giving up. Eventually, I called the Department of Children and Family Services and signed up to be a foster mom. I was transparent; I told the social worker about my last experience, and I explained I ultimately wanted my forever child and signed up for my first parenting class. That was August of 2019. In August of 2020 I got the call. I was on vacation, sitting by a lake reading a magazine, "Sara, can you do siblings?"

"Ummm, no. I only want one. I'm alone, remember? I don't know. I'll take them for a few nights if they have nowhere to go. But I can't do two."

She tells me I can, she knows I can. In my head I'm like, these people will try to get me to do anything, they are desperate. "When do I need to decide?" I asked.

She said, "Can you let me know by 3:00?" It was 11:00 AM.

I ran to my sister. "Of course you can do it," she said, "call her back! You were born to be a mom, we got this, I got you sizzy!"

Fingers shaking, I called her back. I told her yes. She said, "How soon can you get home?"

I said, "I'll leave tonight."

She said, "We are removing them tomorrow morning, we will drop them off at noon."

I hung up the phone, looked at my sister and said, "We gotta go to Walmart." We made a list, and $350 later I was in my car making the four hour drive back to Boston. That night I prepared my home and heart. The next afternoon, a little girl in a faded, tattered Minnie Mouse dress with matted hair and a little boy in a ratty tank top, a diaper, and bare feet showed up on my doorstep. Their teeth were rotted, they were infested with lice and covered in sores and bites, and he had a diaper rash that brought tears to my eyes. The social workers walked them in and dropped off a few duffle bags of too small clothes and three trash bags of bed-bug infested stuffies. The social workers left. And that was it— we were alone. Just like that. Was I a mom?

I don't do bugs. I'm a nurse, I'll deal with HIV, hepatitis, TB, Herpes, but do not, under any circumstances, ask me to deal with bugs. I doused my head in olive oil, got some gloves, put hotel shower caps on their heads and mine, wrapped the car seats in plastic wrap and drove to Lice Treatment Centers of America. There I met my first angel. These kids refused to wear shoes, they were literally not domesticated. This woman was patient and kind. My son was climbing like an actual monkey— hanging from the backs of chairs and light fixtures, and my daughter was hiding under tables. The woman from the lice treatment center just followed the kids to wherever they were and gently and quietly did her thing. She spent hours treating them. She was also a single mom. It was here I first learned about the silent camaraderie; the looks of understanding and patient empathy; the sisterhood of invisible hand holding where we prop eachother up with a nod or a gaze. The lice never came back.

The next day we went shopping— I needed more stuff. How was that possible? I learned self checkout is not for single moms. I am about a third of the way checked out and Monica is standing up in the jump seat of the cart and where are her shoes? Ari, also shoeless, is climbing underneath someone else's cart. Tears sting my eyes, and I try to compose the children and myself. Children who have known me all of 20 hours. The sweet girl working the self checkout station, who couldn't have been a day over nineteen, walks over to me and quietly asks, "Are you a foster mom?"

I said, "Can you tell?"

She said, "I can, let me help you. Do you want me to check you out or help with the kids?"

I handed her my card, whispered my PIN and set out to wrangle the kids. Tears of gratitude, confusion, and worry streamed down my face.

She walked me to our car and shared, "I was a foster kid. Thank you for what you're doing. You're doing great, and they're going to be okay because of you." I think about her so often, whenever it gets really hard. My second angel in as many days.

I took three weeks off to be with them, to bond, and to get to know them— it was the longest, hardest three weeks of my life. They were non-verbal, angry, scared, and hurting. She acted out, and he withdrew. She was demanding and fierce, and he was reserved and timid. She was violent, even scary at times. He was so quiet I would forget he was there. I didn't know what to do. Sometimes I would sit on the floor and cry. I would call my mom and cry. I would sit outside the door in the hallway and cry. I would lay in bed at night and cry. What had I gotten myself into? Was this what I waited for? I am a fixer, and this was unfixable.

I got them enrolled in daycare and started back to work. In an attempt to ward off teenage demons in toddlerhood, I got on a waitlist for therapy. My parents came to visit and fell in love with them. My mom, already four times a grandmother, said, "I thought I would need some time, that it would take me a while to fall in love, but it was the same as with the others. I loved them as soon as I saw them." I don't think my heart was ever so full.

We went home to Philadelphia for Thanksgiving, and they met the whole loud, overbearing, and loving family. It was trial by fire and we survived! They teased and got teased, they played with their cousins and got left out by their cousins, they fell down stairs and climbed trees, they got tickled and ate ice cream for lunch. They were official— they had a seat at the kid's table.

I am not sure when it happened, but between Thanksgiving and Christmas of that year I became "mom." They started calling me mom. I don't really know what they called me before, probably nothing— they didn't really talk. I remember the first time they each said it. For Monica, I was tucking her in and she returned my good night with a sweet and squeaky, "Good night, mom." For Ari, it was pancakes— it's always pancakes. He wanted more pancakes and he said, "Mom, more pancakes." After the holidays, we settled into a routine and things were almost normal. I could fake it in public for about an hour. Like, if we went to the store we could hold together for nearly 60 minutes, and from the outside people might just think I had it together. We were finally #winning.

Let me just hold a side-bar here to tell you what is going on in other parts of the journey. The kids' biological mother and father were already in the process of having their parental rights terminated when they were placed with me. The birth mom had not seen them in 18 months— that was three quarters of Ari's life and half of Monica's. The biological father was in jail for the umpteeth time— his felony record is pages long. In the interim, DCF decided to allow the biological father one last video visit from jail. He was looking smug in his orange jumpsuit and making already broken promises to the kids. He threatened me, reminding me of his power and alluding to his violent past— he's a scary dude. He had multiple felony assaults and access to weapons. He is not an "all talk" kind of a guy.

He was in and out of jail. Each time he was out, I would look over my shoulder, remind the daycare of his presence, and pray for our safety. Two days before Christmas I learned he died in a single car accident—his third in as many months.

Monica has some memories of her birth father. Ari does not. Neither really had a concept of family before the three of us. They understand that lots of kids have dads, and they ask sometimes why they do not. They will grow up believing their dad loved them and he is in heaven. I'm not naive— one day they will read this, and one day they will look for information about him. His arrest record will be there and so will the articles about his car accidents. They can make their own determination about where he is when the time comes.

My children know they are adopted. We talk about their story, the day they came to live with me, and how I am not their first mommy. We talk about how their first mom loved them enough to give them to a mom who could love them the way they needed to be loved. We talk about the people who made us family: the social workers, the lawyers, and the judge. We talk about how some moms are mommies because babies grow in their tummies, and I am a mom because God picked me from all the mommies who wanted children to be their mom because He knew we were a perfect match. I tell them how I prayed and prayed for them, how I waited, and how excited I was when I got the call.

When I first thought about the reality of adopting older children, I thought I would be so sad about missing out on their baby years. And sometimes I am. But in some ways, I am really lucky. My kids remember all their firsts with me. They remember the first time they met their grandparents. They remember our first Christmas. They remember our first vacation. They remember their first s'more. Everything is a first for us, for our family, and they remember it all. That is an incredible gift. So while I might not be their first mom, I am their first everything else. And they are my first true loves.

Adrienne Kennie

Founder of 28th State Business Solutions, LLC

www.Linkedin.com/in/Adrienne-kennie-80ab3327
https://www.facebook.com/adrienne.kennie/
https://www.instagram.com/msnikki_81
https://www.28thstatebusiness.com

Adrienne Kennie was born and raised in Austin, Texas where she currently resides. She received a Bachelor of Science degree in Health Administration from Texas State University and a Masters degree in Business Administration from Concordia University. She also completed the Women's Entrepreneurship program with the Bank of America Institute at Cornell University. She is currently a Management Consultant for a large consulting firm. During her free time, she enjoys spending time with family and friends, making arts and crafts, traveling, writing, and most of all her role as mom to her one-year-old daughter. Adrienne is the CEO of 28th State Business Solutions, LLC, and is currently working on starting her own home health agency and other projects to promote her passion and goals to help others.

REINVENTING MYSELF AND LIVING LIFE ON MY TERMS

By Adrienne Kennie

Unrecognizable

As I stood in the mirror looking at my reflection, I did not recognize myself. My face was not as smooth as it once was, I had gained so much weight that my clothes no longer fit, and I was down to wearing T-shirts and yoga pants daily. The bright eyes and smile that used to light up a room were replaced with dark circles and sadness. At that very moment, I knew that I had lost myself, but it didn't happen overnight. There were signs, and this was the result of something that had been brewing for years.

Crash and Burn

On January 9, 2018, I was sitting in the nail shop getting a manicure after work when I suddenly felt a "bad feeling." As I continued to sit there the feeling did not go away. In fact, I started thinking about my younger brother, and in my heart, I knew that something was wrong with him. I called his cell phone several times, but it went straight to voicemail. A few minutes later, his friend called and stated that my brother was supposed to pick him up from work but never showed up. I left the shop to look for my brother. My brother's friend told us that there was an accident, and we should get to the hospital. When we arrived at the hospital, we were stopped at the entrance by the police. After a series of questions, the police told us that my brother was involved in an accident and unfortunately did not survive. He was pronounced dead at the scene, and his friends that were with him were in critical condition. One passed away the next day and the other was in a coma for six months and passed away. I was distraught. My brother and I were super close. Usually, if you saw one of us the other was not far behind. I didn't take the time to process things, I immediately started handling the arrangements and making sure my family was okay and I pushed through. That was the theme of my life, push through, but this wasn't healthy. In 2019, I lost an aunt, friend, uncle, grandma, and almost lost my dad. Things were extremely difficult, and unfortunately, I wasn't coping or dealing with things, and it was starting to show in my relationships, my work, and my overall body, mind, and spirit. I was drowning and didn't know it.

During this time, I was involved in an on-and-off relationship for ten years. Although this was a long time, there was always something in the pit of my stomach that didn't feel right about the relationship. I never felt that we were progressing as a couple. I wanted a partnership that would lead to marriage, the white picket fence, and children, but it never felt that we would get there. Some obstacles were always in the way. That feeling that I had in the pit of my stomach always prompted the constant "where are we going?" conversations that would lead to arguments, and I would walk away feeling as if my questions were never answered. I felt more alone in the relationship than I ever felt as a single woman, but I always hoped that things would get better if I trusted the process and hung in there. I wasn't happy, and before I knew it, years had flown by and I was nowhere close to being in the relationship that I wanted or being a wife and mother. In February 2021, Texas faced a snowstorm that left thousands without electricity and/or water. I, unfortunately, was one of those people who had no power or running water for five days. It was an uncomfortable position to be in, but the silver lining is that I had five days to think and process the events in my life. I then decided that I wanted to end the relationship and move on.

Positive or Negative

Shortly after the snowstorm, one day I didn't feel quite like myself, and something felt "off." I always had issues with my period, so being late was never a concern for me. In 2015, I was diagnosed with polycystic ovarian syndrome and Hypothyroidism, in addition to having uterine fibroid and endometrial polyps. I honestly didn't think I could have any kids, and I started to mentally prepare for that outcome. I was going back and forth between the ideas of adoption, fertility treatments, and not having any children at all, but I wanted to practice due diligence. I bought a box of pregnancy tests, but when I got home, I was in a hurry and put them away. I was always on the go and that weekend I was busy, so I decided to take the test later. The next morning, I was getting dressed to go to a hair appointment and decided to take the test. I pulled out the box, read the instructions, and took the test. I was running late for the appointment and left the house. I didn't even wait to read the results. Everyone who knows me knows that my hair appointments are important, and I never miss them if possible. I was so sure I wasn't pregnant that I didn't even take the test seriously. I never gave it a second thought and went about my day. After the appointment, I met up with one of my friends and went to dinner. I was out living my best life. When I got home, I walked into the bathroom and suddenly remembered the test when I saw it on the counter. I picked up the stick and as I was about to throw it in the trash can I saw the word "pregnant." "Pregnant? No way!" I ran to grab my keys and purse and headed to the drug store to buy some more tests. I bought four more tests because something had to be wrong. I started drinking water because I was going to be ready to take all four of these tests. After all, in my mind this was impossible. I ended up taking the four tests and they all confirmed a positive pregnancy. At this point, I am in total shock and was hit with the realization that my situation was not what I envisioned: I had just made the decision to end things with my child's father.

The Turning Point

Being a single mom was not what I envisioned, and this came with a level of shame. Here I was, 39 years old and I was worried about what others would think of me because I was pregnant and unmarried. That was a heavy load to carry when I was feeling like a failure to myself and my unborn child. I always knew that I wanted to be a mom and decided that I was going to go through with the pregnancy. Pregnancy came with its own set of challenges. I had several routine appointments, and as time progressed it was discovered that I had anemia and had to set several iron infusion appointments.

Preparing for the baby became my focus, and I started making lists of baby items that I needed and started making purchases. I bought a car seat, stroller, crib, dresser, changing station, and room decorations. I even started buying clothes and other baby accessories. There was a baby shower scheduled, but I felt the intense need to be extra prepared. I won't lie, it was a tough journey and, unfortunately, I did have some unhappy days. I did cry more days than I should have.

One Sunday evening I was at home watching TV when I felt the need to urinate. I went to the restroom and saw that I had some light bleeding and I freaked out. I ended up driving myself to the emergency room, and after being there for four hours I was told that I had a threatened miscarriage and to follow up with my OB/GYN. Thankfully everything was fine, but this did scare me and it made me realize that I needed to calm down from the stress that I was experiencing. I was still working full-time at work, but I made plans to take maternity leave in November 2021.

During my third trimester, I started experiencing swelling and wasn't able to fit in any of my shoes. I was only able to wear crocs. My eyes were always red and glazy, and at times I was short of breath. When I went in for my routine visits, I started having protein in my urine, but my blood pressure was normal so I wasn't diagnosed with preeclampsia. Each day was starting to get harder and harder. My best friend and her mom came to visit me and helped me organize and decorate the baby's room. I was so happy they were there to visit and catch up. On the day that they were leaving, I had a doctor's appointment to attend but made plans to return so that I could see them off before they left.

I rushed into the doctor's office to check-in. At this time, I was 34 weeks and three days into the pregnancy. When the nurse called me back, I settled into the room and she checked my blood pressure. I knew something was wrong when she stated that she would let me sit for a few minutes and recheck my blood pressure. She came back, rechecked my blood pressure, and said she was going to get the doctor. The doctor came in and said that my blood pressure was dangerously high, and I was diagnosed with severe preeclampsia and immediately sent to the hospital. After hours of trying to get my blood pressure down without progress, the fetal medicine doctor determined that it was too dangerous for me and the baby to continue my pregnancy. I had to have an emergency C-section, and thankfully my mom was able to sit next to me during the surgery.

The most amazing sound that I have ever heard was hearing my daughter cry for the first time. My mom was my support and my baby's initial lifeline because I was unstable for three days afterward. I was unable to see or hold my baby during those days. My daughter was in the NICU because she was premature and weighed four pounds and four ounces at birth. Being a NICU parent is tough, but she and I made it through. My daughter was a fighter from the beginning and only stayed in the NICU for eleven days. I was so grateful that we were able to go home and begin our healing.

Healing From the Inside Out

That day in the mirror was a turning point for me. I knew that I needed to make some changes in my life and so I started therapy. I found a counselor and surprisingly she was a good fit. I knew that it was important to find someone that I could connect with for counseling to be successful. I attended weekly sessions with her and spent some time talking through some of the challenges I was facing. To say that I felt a ton of emotions was an understatement. I was adjusting to being a new single mom and still healing from a C-section. I was dealing with postpartum depression, grief, anxiety, and guilt. My goal for counseling was to put my life and myself together because it felt as if everything was falling apart.

The more I talked through my challenges, I realized that I spent countless years not living in my truth. I always did what was expected of me and I was the one that was there for everyone else, but it came at a high cost. I wasn't happy and I wasn't living my purpose. I was always in "go mode" and didn't take the time to take care of myself because I was busy taking care of everyone else. Self-care had become foreign to me, and I didn't know where to start. My counselor suggested that I start journaling. I set aside time in the mornings to journal every day.

One day when I was journaling, I decided to write a list of characteristics, qualities, and things that I needed if and when I decided to be in a relationship again. I truly believe that I spent so much time in unhealthy relationships because I wasn't purposeful in dating or standing firm on what I wanted in a relationship. When you aren't clear about what you want, then there's an opportunity for confusion. I removed pressure from myself to be in a relationship and found peace and happiness in learning how to love myself again, but most of all, I learned how to forgive myself. I also started feeling better about letting family members take care of my daughter for a few hours or a weekend so that I could have some time to myself. At first, I would just clean the house and watch TV but eventually, I started to do things outside of the house such as shopping, grabbing something to eat, spending time with friends, or going for a walk.

When I returned to work, I realized that I needed to find another career opportunity because there was no room for growth. I felt stagnant and needed another opportunity that would enable me to shine fully. After several interviews, I received an offer of employment at another company. After praying, I decided to accept the opportunity and looked forward to the change that this opportunity would provide. I knew that I had made the right decision to leave. I started to feel overwhelmed by all of the changes that were happening in my life, but I soon learned that we grow as individuals when we are in situations that are uncomfortable and get through them. I also felt a sense of peace that I had not felt in years. I was at peace with myself, my life, my ability to be a good mom, my career, and I started feeling like my life was aligning with my god-given purpose. I am starting to challenge myself to do things that are scary and uncomfortable so that I can continue to grow. The best role that I have ever had in my life is being a mother. I am *determined* to be the best mother that I can be for my daughter and knew that she needed a mom that was whole inside and out. My mission is to provide a healthy and loving environment for her to grow up in, and I am making strides to fulfill that mission.

The greatest lesson that I learned from my late brother was that it doesn't matter what others think of me, what ultimately matters is what I think of myself. He always said that I needed to live life on my terms and that's what I intend to do. If you want to follow my journey, I can be reached at:

www.linkedin.com/in/Adrienne-kennie-80ab3327
https://www.instagram.com/msnikki_81
https://www.28thstatebusiness.com

Cindy Witteman

Founder & CEO of Driving Single Parents Inc.

https://www.Facebook.com/Cindy.Witt.902
https://www.instagram.com/Cindy.Witteman
https://linktr.ee/Cindy.Witteman

My name is Cindy Witteman, I live in San Antonio, Texas. I am the Founder and CEO of Driving Single Parents Incorporated which is a 501(c)3 Non-Profit. I am a former single parent with a total of 6 kids, 1 grandson, and 2 granddaughters on the way. I love to travel, spend time with family, and am a pilot in progress. I have a passion for giving back and helping single parents regain their independence. Driving Single Parents Inc. will soon celebrate 5 years in existence while successfully changing the lives of multiple single-parent families. DSP & affiliates have provided these families with reliable vehicles at NO cost to them. These parents have gone on to have success stories of their own by using the car as a tool to transform their single-parent struggles into a thing of the past while creating a bright future with lots of potential for their children.

IT'S BETTER TO COME FROM A BROKEN HOME THAN IT IS TO GROW UP IN ONE

By Cindy Witteman

I grew up in Texas, raised primarily by a single mom. She was disabled and did not work for most of my childhood so we didn't have much and often lacked food, electricity, or running water. It was rare that we had a vehicle to get to the grocery store, doctor's appointments, or even school. However, I always had a go-getter type of attitude and often tried to find creative ways to solve problems. I learned how to earn money and budget at an early age. I remember going up to strangers as a small child and asking how they got those nice shoes, cool clothes, fancy cars, or gorgeous homes. I would always get the same answer: an excellent job. I remember thinking, "Geez, I gotta get me one of those as soon as possible." Unfortunately, I was too young to start working at that time. When I was in my teens and in a committed relationship, a plan popped into my head. I had figured it out... The way I would get myself into a better situation was to get married, start my happily ever after, and leave all those struggles behind.

Or so I thought...

Soon I married the man I thought would give me my happily ever after. My husband had a job, we lived in a fifth-wheel trailer, had our own vehicle, and all the essentials I lacked growing up. Our first little girl was born, and we were both over the moon with excitement when we brought her home from the hospital. He was a picture-perfect first-time dad, loving and kind. He would hold her for hours and hated leaving for work. Everything was going well. It was never perfect, but what marriage is?

Shortly after the birth of our daughter, there was a dramatic shift. I was never able to figure out precisely what happened. It was just like the experts say: it started off gradually with name-calling, pushing, and emotional abuse. Over time he started drinking, and once we were alone he would just snap! The violence continued to escalate throughout the marriage. As the years passed, we welcomed two more little girls to the family, and as time continued to slip by I started to realize this was not going to get better, that I was truly stuck, and it was probably going to be forever...

"It's better to come from a broken home than it is to grow up in one."

I was watching Dr. Phil while folding laundry when I first heard this quote. I immediately acted as if those words were being spoken directly to me. I jumped up, grabbed a basket of clothes, a bag of diapers, and my daughters, and left. I never turned back. I realized by avoiding becoming a single mom I was inadvertently dragging my daughters through hell and teaching them it was okay to allow someone to treat us this way.

So there I was, 21 years old and running out of a toxic and abusive marriage with three little girls toward something I had feared since childhood: single parenthood. Coming from a single-parent home myself, I had always promised I would never end up in this situation. I remember thinking, "This cannot be happening—not to me, and not to my little girls!

As I braced myself to get in the car—ready to escape this terrible reality—I heard that awful voice repeating all the horrible things I had been brainwashed to believe. "You are stupid, ugly, worthless, trash, and nobody wants you."

Something made me snap back into reality as I strapped my five-month-old into her car seat. I took a deep breath, got into the car, and headed toward a very uncertain future. During that car ride, I vowed to prove to myself I could get through this, was worth more, and would teach my daughters how to become strong independent women with heart, ambition, and self-worth.

My future wasn't all sunshine and rainbows right away. Before I knew it, I was working two jobs and going to school to better my education. I drove my Ford Escort all over the city—from school to work to babysitters and back. I would come home, tuck the girls in bed, exhausted, and get up and do it all again the next day. I put in the hard work until I had my own place, a car in my name, and hugs from my daughters after walking the stage at my college graduation.

By 2008, I had secured a career path in the legal field, quit my second job, and after years of renting, started construction on our first home. A brand-new home that would be just ours, safe, without pain, fear, or limitations.

As time passed, I became established and more stable. I would often dream that one day I would be able to give back and help other single parents escape the stigma and overcome all the obstacles that life would undoubtedly put in their path.

Years later I met my best friend and the man of my dreams. I was fortunate to add him and his children to our family, which gave us a grand total of six kiddos to love and care for. With each day, I learned to love myself and value my worth. The strength I gained through all the hardship really helped me become a confident and successful woman with a lot to offer in this life. I knew I needed to use it to help other struggling people, but I didn't know how.

I often thought back to the struggles I faced as a single parent, and what ultimately helped me to become successful— my own strength, a few encouraging words, and the need I had for that little Ford Escort.

I was at dinner when it suddenly all came together. I jumped out of my chair and announced to my then-fiance that I was going to start a nonprofit and give away cars to single parents in need! After all, It would have been impossible to maintain two jobs and go to college while getting my little ones to school without my vehicle.

My fiancé immediately glared across the table at me with a half-joking and half-serious look on his face, and said, "Sit down, you are not giving away cars!" He could immediately see the possibility of major liability issues rushing through his mind all at once. But to me, it all made perfect sense. I remember excitedly telling our server my idea while Andrew looked on with a grin—not fully realizing the true scope and scale of what was about to jump out of my head and into reality.

The next morning, I woke up super early and built the website before he even crawled out of bed. When he woke, I told him what I had accomplished. "Wow," he said. "You're really doing this!" The look of pride on his face told me I had all the support I needed for my new venture.

I dove into researching everything I needed to know about how to start a nonprofit. I spent many hours reading books, searching the web, and talking to anyone who I thought might have insight into how the nonprofit could grow and become successful. With my research indicating there are one and a half million exempt nonprofits in the United States alone, it's not surprising that thousands fail each year. Forbes states fifty percent will hit a wall in the first twelve months. Therefore, I needed to learn how to ensure that would not happen to Driving Single Parents Inc. I was fortunate that I was already surrounded by people who had a lot to offer, whether it be advice, support, or willingness to volunteer their time and expertise. It was less than a month after I founded the nonprofit before the first car giveaway on April 1st, 2017. The vehicle went to a very deserving single-parent family. I was so proud that I was able to purchase that first vehicle with my own hard-earned money.

Fast forward, I have maintained my career of almost 15 years in the legal field. I am proud that my current position helps other survivors have the ability to access the services available to report domestic violence.

Driving Single Parents Inc. (DSP) will soon celebrate five years in existence while successfully changing the lives of multiple families. DSP and partners have provided these families with reliable vehicles at no cost to them! They have gone on to enroll in higher education programs, get promoted at work, graduate from college, start new careers, and some have even become homeowners themselves. The future's so bright, and I am thrilled to share that sometimes the hard road makes you stronger. Those experiences can serve as stepping stones to help you give back and grow into the amazing person you will become. You can truly do anything you put your mind to. Never let anyone convince you otherwise.

If you have questions or would like to learn more, please feel free to reach out:

Driving Single Parents Inc.
Cindy Witteman
Founder/CEO
Info@DrivingSingleParents.org
DrivingSingleParents.org

Michele Meza

Luksi Coaching & Consulting, LLC
Certified Mindset Coach and Branding Solutions Expert

www.linkedin.com/in/coachmicheled
https://www.facebook.com/luksiconsulting
https://www.instagram.com/coachmicheled/
https://www.instagram.com/luksiconsulting/
https://www.luksiconsulting.com

For over 28 years, Michele Meza, also known as, Coach Michele D, has been a noteworthy leader in business and academia industries and is known for her work as the Branding Strategist at Luksi Coaching & Consulting; Michele has been featured in several well-known industry publications, books, and podcasts.

Coach Michele D has been honored with multiple recognitions, including a national leadership award "Native 40 under 40" for her contributions and expertise in business and Native American communities. She is formally trained in Organizational Leadership, holds a MBA, a Bachelor of Science degree in Entrepreneurship from Bacone College, and is extensively trained in strategic leadership. She holds certifications as a Business Process Manager, Green Belt in Lean Six Sigma, REBT Mindset Coach, and Emotional Intelligence Transformational Coach. Michele is involved in real estate and resides in Tulsa, Oklahoma. She's passionate about generational wealth and breaking the stigma against single motherhood.

HOPE AFTER HEARTBREAK

By Michele Meza

Introduction

Chances are, you don't know me, but I have a story to tell. A raw, real-life story of finding hope after a lifetime of heartbreak. When this story finds you, my goal is for it to encourage you, inspire you, motivate you, and give you the grit to push through whatever challenges you're facing. I want you to know that you are loved, you are seen, and you are heard. Most importantly, may you find the courage and strength to raise those babies or grandbabies and find yourself again.

I had life figured out at a young age; a life carefully planned out like all the princess movies I watched as a little girl. The perfect life where I find the man of my dreams, have the dreamiest wedding known to man, settle into our careers, then plan out our family and grow old together. But somehow, life just didn't turn out the way I had planned.

Generational Cycles of Trauma

Before I understood what generational cycles were all about, I found myself going down the same path my parents went on. I had a very unstable upbringing because my parents were gypsies. Technically, it was just my dad. Dad was the oldest of six; his dad died young, which left all the responsibility of taking care of the family on his shoulders. I'm not sure where the generational trauma began, but I definitely know where it continued.

Let's dive into trauma cycle number two. I swear my beautiful, strong mama was born tough. She literally was the face of adversity. Her mother, my grandmother, was a Native American child born in 1914, and was part of the Indian removal. My grandma also lived through the Great Depression, the Dust Bowl, cancer, divorce, domestic abuse, and much more. The first cycle of divorce began with my grandma and grandpa. My mom was the youngest of four. Shortly after mom was born in a little community in Southern Oklahoma, famine hit and the family packed up and moved to the promised land, also known as California.

Most years, I ended up taking care of myself as a latchkey kid. My dad was in and out of my life so often, and I assumed everyone's childhood was the same. When my dad did come back into our lives, it was chaos. There was lots of fighting, abuse of every kind, alcohol, and threats of ending lives. Oftentimes, I didn't know what to do but escape into the beautiful countryside. That particular landscape included Oklahoma fields, Arizona sand dunes and cacti, and Arkansas rivers. I was 14 when my dad swore to my mom that he would stay. She believed him.

Even though dad had penned himself as a "family man" now, his habits turned into addiction; He was an alcoholic. In his eyes, he was fine because he could get up and go to work, but in his downtime, things got worse. I remember coming home late one evening after basketball practice. I was so excited to tell mom and dad that I made the team— first string! I just knew I'd make them so proud. I even secretly thought that maybe if my dad was happy, then he wouldn't drink and abuse us. Instead of winning his heart, he told me that he wasn't going to pay for anything of mine. Determined to not allow his hurtful words to penetrate my heart, I got a job and never asked him for anything ever again.

Wrong Way

By the ripe age of 18, I hated the world, and I allowed my hurt to make my decisions. I deeply loved this one guy, but he chased every other girl in addition to me. Months went by, and my anger grew. I didn't really care about myself, let alone anyone else. I was focused on leaving that one-horse town. College was great! I lived my best life and focused on my future; a future of prosperity and a life I left behind.

It was the spring of 2000 when I met my college sweetheart. A few months later, he became possessive and controlling—all the things in my dad that I swore I wouldn't accept. But, I was focused on making money. I was the first to go to college and graduate out of both sides of my family. I planned to be the first millionaire, come hell or high water. Secretly, I knew I had to get away from this guy I thought I loved. He was too jealous of me. I just wasn't going to put up with it like my mama did. I applied for several jobs throughout the USA. I took the first job offered to me, which was not too far from my college town, but was far enough away that people wouldn't make the effort to visit me.

Evil's Reign

After moving away, I felt like I was in control for the first time in my life. I had it all together and was on the path to pursuing my dreams. I felt unstoppable; I had abandoned a life of poverty and fled from my controlling parents. I had a new apartment and owned my world. However, on a cold day in January, my life changed forever. I recall pulling up to my assigned parking spot at my apartment, exhausted from the day. I slowly opened my car door and gathered my things. As I stepped out of my car, I was abruptly slammed to the ground. I had no idea what was happening; was I going to die? Who was so angry at me to do this? All these questions were going through my mind as I tirelessly defended my petite 90-pound frame. I fought him until I was knocked unconscious. The next day, I tried to process what happened and realized that the apartment complex had security cameras. I attempted to share what happened with the apartment manager; however, she quickly interrupted me and assured me nothing like this happens at her facility. It was at that moment that I realized nobody believed me. If a complete stranger didn't believe me, how would anyone I knew believe me? At that point, I made the decision to never tell anyone. I continued to have nightmares and decided that I needed to move back to my college town, where it felt like home. After all, I couldn't go "home" to my parents. I didn't have a job or anywhere to live, so I decided to move into my college sweetheart's house with him. His reaction was expected; so happy I'd come to my senses and returned to where I "needed to be."

Beauty for Ashes

A few months later, I got sick in the mornings. I was so naive and ignorant, having come from a generation who "didn't talk about it"—or anything for that matter. A friend of mine mentioned that I might be pregnant. I was scared to death. Pregnant? Wait—my life was planned out. How could this happen? She convinced me to take a pregnancy test. Low and behold, it was positive. How did I feel? I felt nothing. You see, I forced myself to block out bad things that occurred throughout my life—that's how I survived—and that's exactly what I did. I didn't really understand what was going on. I didn't process what happened to me. My mind just couldn't connect the dots as to how I was now carrying a child. I started showing, so I knew I had to tell my sweetheart. I had lied to myself thinking he'd be so happy, but, instead, he was the opposite. Then came the accusations; he just knew he was right about me cheating on him.

After many arguments with him, and the consensus of my friend group, I decided the best decision was to terminate the pregnancy. When I walked through those doors, I was confident in my decision. A few minutes later, a young girl walked out, I'm guessing about twelve, along with her parents. I will never forget the look on her face. I've never seen fear, devastation, and shame rolled into one look. As they walked out, I threw up and ran out of that place. I swore to God that I would never visit that place again.

My original due date was on Thanksgiving of that year—also, my older brother's birthday. The due date came and went. I had worked up to forty weeks. I went in on a Monday to be induced, but ended up having my beautiful eight-pound, four-ounce baby girl four days later. My delivery was a medical book's version of what goes wrong. Not only did I flat line, but my baby almost died. Somehow, by the grace of God, my baby and I survived.

When my beautiful gem was just three weeks old, my sweetheart decided he wasn't cut out to be a dad. He called my parents and sent me on my way; in the middle of winter with at least one inch of ice and three inches of snow on the ground. I was so confused. Here I was, a twenty-four-year-old new mother with a huge hole in my incision from a botched emergency C-section, driving three hours to where my parents were living during that time in hazardous conditions. I remember thinking: how did I end up here? Why me? What's next? Months later, my mom came clean and told me that my sweetheart had confirmed his accusation: my beautiful, blue-eyed baby girl wasn't his. Indeed, she wasn't. I'll never forget that day either. It's funny how our minds rationalize things during fight or flight; our illusions become our truth and our reality. It was at that pivotal moment that I was forced to accept the crime that happened to me. Some random, evil man stole the life right out of me. My hate for the world, especially men, resurfaced. What was I going to tell everyone? Up until a few years ago, I felt and re-lived the shame and experienced the stigma and public disgust tied to single and unwed mothers over and over again.

Devil in Disguise

Years later, I'd moved on and moved to a new state—new beginnings. I was at the height of my career, with a beautiful little girl who adored me, and under the security of my new life. Until I met my husband. He was super charming and handsome, and I dated him for a couple of years before I introduced him to my daughter. He adored her and she approved of him. I finally felt like my life was coming together to where I wanted it to be.

Fast forward to our first year of marriage. We had just found out that we were having a girl! He wanted a boy, but was happy anyway. A few days later, I was in a horrible car accident that left me paralyzed from the neck down. Somehow, I managed to not miscarry my beautiful baby girl. The next few months would be challenging like never before. My husband went from just going to work and coming home, to working, caring for his daughter and mine, our unborn baby, and me. He despised it. That's when the real him came out. He began to no longer hide his addiction to drinking, sex, and women.

When I had my second baby girl, by the grace of God, I regained most of my feeling back in half of my body. It was truly a miracle that I not only carried my baby to term, but delivered a healthy baby while recovering from paralyzation. During those months of paralyzation, I knew I had two choices: give up and accept life as a quadriplegic, or to keep fighting. I chose to fight. Along with my stubbornness, *lots* of time with God, and speaking scriptures and affirmations over myself, I was able to feel most of my body. For once, I felt like I conquered defeat; I won over the enemy. Within the same breath, I knew I was dancing with the devil. In addition to physical manifestations of demons, my husband made sure I paid for what happened to me and what he had to give up during that time. What quickly went from degrading words, turned quickly into violence.

As I barricaded myself and my two girls in one of their rooms, I knew this wasn't the life I had envisioned for them. That morning, when he awoke from his drunken slumber, I made his lunch and sent him off to work. At that moment, I had to make a quick decision: do I stay and be dead six months later with the possibility of him taking my children off somewhere for good, or do I quietly escape to a safe haven? Well, I made the decision to leave, and I haven't looked back. The transition was rough; there were months of living in my car and staying under the radar just praying he wouldn't find us and kill me. I begged God to help me. I begged him to teach me how to break the never-ending cycles of abuse that my family had. What I found was that God fulfills His promises. He restores generations of loss and puts us back together again. And in that, there's hope.

Hope Restored

As I reflect on our lives after my decision to escape the prison we were in ten years ago, I'm glad I made the right choice. Our hope and faith were restored. My mindset is renewed, and my body is healed. I traded my shame for my testimony. Our lives look completely different from what I had planned. Even though my girls are growing up in a single parent home, they are loved, and they have what they need. They are able to come home to a house of healing, hope, and peace—a place of restoration. They've witnessed the transformation in me, which encourages them to go for their dreams. Not only were our hearts healed, but my desires and prayers are continuing to be fulfilled. I came from a destitute place to a land of prosperity. I'm living proof that there's hope after heartbreak. And, my friend, it's available to you too.

Do you need help renewing your mindset or taking the leap of faith like I did and paving your own path to entrepreneurship and freedom? Let's have a conversation!

What I do:

www.luksiconsulting.com

Let's Stay Connected:

https://www.facebook.com/luksiconsulting
https://www.instagram.com/coachmicheled/
https://www.instagram.com/luksiconsulting/
https://www.linkedin.com/in/coachmicheled/

Denise Hernandez

Shipt
Personal Shopper

https://www.instagram.com/sweet.sunflower.fairy/

Denise Hernandez is a new, and upcoming author who wants to share her story and help others by doing so.

Denise Hernandez was born in Chicago, IL, and raised in Miami, FL. She studied Early Childhood Education at Florida International University. She has always dreamt of becoming an author, writing children's books to help teach her students in the classroom. She has been writing in diaries for as long as she can remember, and she has a deep love of reading and learning. She began writing her personal story in 2017, after a traumatic event that left her yearning to help others. When she is not writing, Denise loves to watch movies, play pool, and meet new people. Her favorite destination is Disney World and dreams of traveling to Paris. She has two children and is a personal shopper. She currently lives in Miami with her children, significant other, and their dog.

THIN LINE BETWEEN HEAVEN AND HELL

By Denise Hernandez

I ran with my car keys, tears streaming down my face, not knowing where I was going or what I was going to do. My mind was cloudy, my heart was pounding a mile a minute, and in between sobs, I would try to catch my breath.

I was screaming to myself in the car "I NEED HELP! I NEED HELP!" Over and over again until I got lost. I rerouted myself somehow and found that I was now parking at the ER at the local hospital.

Still very hysterical, I walked in and went to the counter and all I could manage to say was, "I need help. I want to kill myself…"

I was diagnosed officially in 2017 with panic disorder and major depressive disorder. I have dealt with anxiety and depression for as long as I can remember. At the age of seven, my family moved from a tiny, safe town in Illinois, to crazy Miami, Florida, and I was not happy about it. In Miami, I was constantly getting bullied for my short stature and my big, "Dumbo"-looking ears. That became my nickname, and because of this, I came to dislike the Disney movie greatly.

I began dating for the first time in college. My boyfriend was not a very nice person, but I thought that was love. I moved to Virginia with him after he accepted a job post-graduation. We broke up after a year when he admitted to cheating, and I decided to take the Amtrak home to Miami.

During my 16-hour train ride, I felt sick the whole time. Once I arrived in Sanford, I now had the task of driving about five hours south to Miami alone. On the way, I realized Father's Day was coming and began to think about what I would get my dad. Suddenly, I had this sense that I would not need to get him anything. I knew he had died overnight. I began driving faster and faster, and once I arrived home after a very long 24 hours, I received the news from my mother that my dad had indeed passed away the evening I was on the train from a heart attack.

Just six years later, I also lost my mom. She had made an appointment with a cardiologist but never made it because she died of a heart attack in her sleep. My son was only five months old when she passed.

These deaths were a turning point in my life where, because of my anxiety and depression, I could no longer function for about a month. I had friends tell me that I needed to learn to be alone with my son during this time… that I needed to shape up and be strong. How could I be strong when my entire foundation had fallen apart and I no longer had a solid ground to walk on anymore?

I had already been dealing with postpartum depression since my son was born. The hospital even had me see a therapist two days after my son was born. I was in the hospital for a week, because I developed Bell's Palsy due to the stress of the end of the pregnancy and the whole birthing process which took 30 hours and an emergency C-section. There were days I wanted to end it all—just leave my son with his father and be done with this world. I wanted to run away. Was I even ready to be a mom? I hid these thoughts from everyone because I was afraid they would take my baby away from me, even though I wasn't quite sure I could handle this overwhelming responsibility that lay in front of me. This was just the beginning of how my life took a drastic turn that no one had expected.

The year 2017 started pretty normal. I was working at my good friend's home daycare, and was lucky enough to have my almost two-year-old daughter with me daily. At that point, she had only been apart from me one weekend in her life.

My health was the only thing at the moment that was bothering me. My husband, Chris, and I were taking Dave Ramsey's Financial Peace

University class at the local church and I felt I needed more income. I found a lady on Facebook who was an entrepreneur for a wellness company a month into 2017 and we started a conversation about my ongoing health issues: how I was always sick with throat infections/stomach bugs/colds and I was tired of it all. Before long, I was an independent contractor and needed to spike up my new wellness business! I created a blog and a Facebook page and began to promote my business on my personal Facebook page. I was very happy to have gotten so much support from my friends. However, I felt this still wasn't enough and soon another friend approached me about another company called "Usborne Books and More." I figured, "Wow, this would be easy to sell! All my friends have kids give years of age and younger, who doesn't love children's books?!" So I began my journey into my third job. Needless to say, I began to feel very overwhelmed.

All the while, I was drowning. I never let on how I felt, but I was starting to pull away little by little. I was always on the verge of crying, an anxious panic-driven person who was barely able to keep herself together, let alone take care of two very young children.

One evening in August, I decided my family needed to have a budget meeting. According to Dave Ramsey, we should be having weekly meetings, yet it had now been months since we spoke about our finances. I had also stopped the other two independent contractor jobs, as I was completely burnt out. My son was about to enter VPK, and my daughter was no longer going to be joining us at the daycare; she was starting real school at the age of almost two and a half.

During this meeting, my husband did not want to disclose his credit card information. I pressed on and said that we needed to be on the same page about this. His response was, "But this has nothing to do with you. It's my card." That statement started a fire in me that would not be let out for a very long time to come…

Finally, he agreed and disclosed the amount of $18,000 on the credit card. I was floored. What in the world could he be spending this money on? Reluctantly, he agreed to let me go through the entire account and add up the expenses. His hobby was costing him $10,000 alone. My anxiety shot through the roof. I only saw red at that point.

The next day at the daycare, suicidal thoughts swarmed my head. As I took the toddlers on our daily walk in the stroller, tears wouldn't stop streaming down my face. Krystal, who owned the daycare, had no idea the angst I was feeling. I only let one person know, my amazing friend, Emilia*. She told me if I did not calm down, she would call the police on me because she did not want anything happening to me. I told her I just needed to vent about it but that I would be okay. Krystal could sense I was not feeling okay but didn't press me further because I insisted I was okay.

A few months went by and I did not feel any better. I was crying alone in the bathroom, wondering where I went wrong in life. How did my kids deserve a mother like me who couldn't even handle money correctly and who was incapable of being there when they needed me? I would turn to the suicide hotline text number time and time again. I was on Sertraline at the time, 50-mg dosage, and often I thought, "What if I just take all these pills at once? Will that end my suffering?" But then I was too scared of throwing up all that medication, so I never did.

November 2017 changed everything …

I finally had a tonsillectomy, after so many years of contracting strep throat every few months. However, that surgery was a nightmare. I could not speak. I could not sneeze. I could not laugh. I could not move! I could barely drink liquids. They gave me Vicodin but I was too afraid of getting addicted to it, so I only took it once and it made me fall asleep. Oh, that heavy sleep was exactly what I needed to get through this nightmare.

On November 10, I had to get over the pain, as my husband and I had planned a Disney trip for two for his birthday. It was Mickey's Very Merry Christmas Party and I was excited. However, during the actual event, I still could not speak well and was in pain from my monthly cycle which just happened to come two days prior. Yet, all the while, my thoughts kept surrounding themselves on what would happen if I was no longer on Earth. Would the kids be okay? Would Chris be okay? Would anyone even care? Wouldn't the kids be better off without me?

On November 11, we walked into the house after our one-day vacation. I had been singing in my head silently all day, "…It'll be alright, Still I hear you say, you want to end your life… Now and again we try to just stay alive. Maybe we'll turn it all around, 'cause it's not too late, it's never too late.." from Three Days Grace.

I turned to my four-year-old son and asked if he was ready to go have dinner with daddy. He threw himself on the couch and yelled, "NO!!" For some reason, this triggered me to the point of no return. That was the evening I admitted myself into the hospital as a Baker Act patient.

I spent about eleven days between two facilities that dealt with people who needed help. I was feeling numb to the world. I desperately wanted to get out of there but did not want to return to reality. Once I left the first facility and got transferred back to the main hospital, things seemed to get better. I had a roommate and we bonded very quickly. I also made friends with another man going through a detox named, James*. As we went through the days together, the three of us got very close. James and I started to talk more in-depth about feelings, and he wrote me a letter. He called me "green eyes," as we both had green eyes and I felt a closeness with him that I had not felt before. Maybe it was because there was someone who finally understood my pain.

Eventually, I came back home, and I was still very much out of touch with reality. I started seeing James more often. He eventually broke it off with me, however, knowing I was married and did not want to be the "home wrecker." Kissing was as far as that relationship went, but it tore me apart inside.

My depression deepened yet again and I felt I was in a black hole that I couldn't crawl out of. Now I had no job, my marriage seemed to be on the rocks, and I was barely hanging by a thread. One tug and that would be it... that would be the end of Denise Hernandez.

In December, I decided that I needed to get out of the house, and I remembered the grocery delivery company my friend Krystal used for the daycare. I looked up how to get a job there and interviewed. I found out I passed and now had a job! This would force me to get out of bed, speak to people, and maybe feel productive in society once again. This job honestly saved me.

Fast forward to June 2018. I finally sat down with Chris and explained that I wanted a divorce and that I already had the paperwork. That began my journey into single motherhood.

The comments I received about this ordeal were as follows: "You just want to be a part-time mom", and "Your time in the psych ward was a nice little vacation for you"... just to name a few. I felt more alone than ever. Chris and I decided to start our new 50-50 schedule right away to get the children used to being with only one parent at a time. I was scared shitless. I could barely handle the kids when I was with my husband, how would I be able to handle them by myself? I told myself that I was strong and worthy to be their mother. I prayed and prayed. I looked to the heavens at my parents, who had been deceased for quite some time now... and I found strength.

I would make plans ahead of time on my weekends with my kids, making sure to always be out and about because it somehow felt easier to be out in public than in the house between the walls which held all my secrets and inner thoughts. My friend support system was nearly non-existent until I met Rori, another single mom of two young kids. She has been my rock throughout everything in my life, and how I have overcome the doubts and questions in my mind that still sometimes irk me.

It's been five years since my breakdown. Writing and reliving through the anxieties, depression, and how I have found strength through God and my children stirred up many emotions in me. I found some parts that made me angry, sad, regretful, overjoyed, and overwhelmingly grateful. Grateful for all the experiences that have led me to who I am today—a woman who has overcome obstacles and no longer takes precious moments for granted. "Every day may not be good… but there's something good in every day," quotes Alice Morse Earle.

I could not have grown and become the strong, independent woman I am today without becoming a single mother. I find inspiration all around me to show my children that through God, prayer, and loving yourself you can accomplish anything you set your heart to. I hope to do the same for you.

Please feel free to contact me at:
Denise Hernandez
Denisemhernandez83@gmail.com

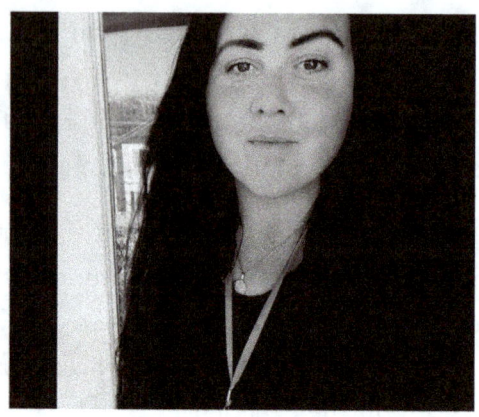

Sarah Miller

CEO & Founder of Sarah Miller & Co

https://www.facebook.com/hisarahmiller
https://www.instagram.com/hisarahmiller
https://www.linkedin.com/in/hisarahmiller
www.sarahmillerco.com

Sarah Miller is currently an Operations Manager, author, speaker, and dog-lover. She loves to express her creativity and love through food by creating new recipes to share with her family and friends. After struggling financially for three years and having to lean on the government for assistance, she was able to find her path to financial independence and earn a six-figure income without a college degree. Sarah enjoys being immersed in cultures that are not native to her own. She's a coffee aficionado, a foodie, an avid reader, and is always up for a challenge. Her interests are amplified by a deep wanderlust, so she and her son travel every chance they get. Sarah hopes that by sharing her story with other single mothers, they will gain the confidence and courage to take the actionable steps to get to where they want to be in life.

HAVE FAITH, MAKE A PLAN

By Sarah Miller

I'll never forget the day when I truly felt free from the baggage of my past. I walked outside where I could have some privacy and took a deep breath as I dialed the number to the local SNAP office. A woman answered the phone and asked what she could do for me. Filled with excitement, I thanked her (even though I knew it wasn't her directly) for helping my family the last few years and said that I had recently received an increase in income and then asked her to cancel my benefits. It was a quiet win for me as I didn't really let anyone know that I had been leaning on the government for support the last few years. I did a celebratory twirl, walked to the corner store to get a coffee, then went back to my office.

You may be wondering how I ended up here…

I was raised in an upper-middle-class family. We never went without anything. My parents divorced when I was very young, but they were both involved in my life. I was competitive in everything I did—sports, music, schoolwork, and modeling. I was your typical Type A personality.

Here I was, 23 years old with a three-year-old, celebrating canceling my food stamps and WIC. Yes, I'm sure the last few years would have been easier financially if I asked my parents for support or asked to live with them, but I was Mommy. I was going to be the one to support my child, not my parents. I got my son and I in this mess, so I would be the one in control of getting us out of it. At that point, I had just been hired on to a full-time position making $17 per hour from being a contractor making $11 per hour. I remember seeing my offer letter: $17.27 per hour, two weeks of vacation time, a week of sick time, medical benefits… This was amazing! I remember thinking to myself that it was so much money that I could use to provide for my son and myself and that I didn't have to be on assistance anymore. As soon as I accepted the employment offer, I walked outside to call the SNAP office. Those few years on assistance were such an embarrassing time for me, but I had to do it. At one point, I only had $5 and we needed things from the store, but I couldn't get them for us. I tried to get help with daycare, but $11/hour was considered too high of an income for daycare assistance, so I had to figure out how to pay $800/month for someone to care for my child while I worked for $1,500 per month, which left me with $700 for my (thankfully small) $300 mortgage and other bills. It was tight. I wasn't receiving child support and was not going to ask my parents for money. This topic came up during one of my venting sessions with my dad and he said, "*You need to apply for food stamps, the government has these programs for a reason. It's for people in your situation who are trying to live and do better, and who just need help right now. It's not a forever thing. And don't worry about taking money from the government, you'll be paying it back plus more in taxes once you get your career going.*" That made me feel a little better—and he was right, too, darn taxes! I put my pride aside and got help. However, I did go to different towns from where I lived to do my grocery shopping. I was ashamed.

One day in particular is embedded in my memory. I had a cart full of groceries and was at the checkout line, and my stupid SNAP card or WIC envelope or something was in my car and not in my wallet where it should have been. I panicked, told the cashier, and instead of giving a tiny bit of grace, she looked at me with disgust, then looked at the customers behind me in line and said very loudly to them, "She forgot her welfare checks in her car. She has to go get them, so it'll be a few minutes... Sorry for the inconvenience!" I was so humiliated.

Around the time that I was hired by my employer, I had also started a second job at a new restaurant bartending and waitressing. After a few months of working both jobs, I started to realize that I was making *a lot* of money: $17/hour plus an extra $700-$1,200 per week in tips from the restaurant. It was a nice change; I felt really proud that I could pay for my son's daycare, buy groceries, buy us new clothes instead of second-hand, afford our condo downtown, and hire a personal trainer to work out with me five days per week.

So when is it that I became a single mom? *That* started before my son was born. It was a high-school sweetheart's first "love" situation. We started dating when I was 16, and I spent the next four years seeking approval and love from a sadistic narcissist; although, I didn't really know at the time what "love" was supposed to look like. In some twisted way, my mind thought that his trying to control me was a sign of love. In retrospect, all that time was a big chaotic mess. Three months into our relationship, I was pregnant. Shortly after I found out, I got an abortion—not my choice, but it happened. Things got a little crazy when he found out, and that's when the abuse started. I had to get a short-term protective order against him for the constant harassment. But, once the order ended, we found our way back together. Then it got worse. At that point, I was full of guilt; all I wanted was my baby and to be a mom. We wanted to work, I think, but we were so young. It doesn't make sense to me now when I look back on it through a wiser lens. We tried, but we brought out the absolute worst in each other. The verbal and physical aggression was intense and kept getting worse. After I graduated high school, we moved into an apartment together and were pregnant the following year. I bought a house, and my dad put his life on hold to do the renovations so we could live there. I spent time getting the baby's nursery together, washing his little outfits, organizing his things, and getting ready for him. We were finally doing it; we were making our "perfect life."

The dreams of this life I had over the last four years eventually shattered. The arguments kept getting bigger and louder. He couldn't control his temper. Instead of us building a life, I walked away from an abusive engagement. It took one final push to the floor when I was eight months pregnant; that's when I decided enough was enough. Something triggered in my mama-bear brain, and I wasn't going to allow him to harm me while carrying the baby. I left that night and came back the next day with my dad to get some of my things. He had taken EVERY.SINGLE.THING. that I owned for the baby that was going to be delivered in less than three weeks. All I had was an empty crib and a rug. No mattress, no blankets, no clothes, diapers, bottles, binkies—nothing. I ended up moving into my old bedroom at my dad's house, set up the baby's crib in my room, and made it work. I had my son a few weeks later. We stayed with my dad for the first six months of his life.

Staying with my dad gave me a safe space to take care of the baby and get on my feet. I needed to heal from the trauma bond that was finally breaking, so I enrolled in a domestic violence support group and met twice a week with other women who had gone through similar experiences in their relationships. It was a safe space to get support and it gave me the tools to change my mindset and realize that what had been going on over the course of the last few years was not healthy or normal behavior.

My ex eventually met our son when he was six months old and started seeing him on a consistent-ish basis until the baby was almost four years old. Interactions with my ex eventually morphed back into a twisted darkness, and I had to get a restraining order for my son and myself due to threats and harassment from him. Regardless of the lack of involvement from his father, I vowed to give my son the best life I could. I was going to make sure that he had the opportunity to experience everything, and that I would raise him to be kind, polite, respectful, and that he would always be surrounded by positivity and love.

I'd say we've accomplished that pretty well so far. Brady is AMAZING, and I'm not just saying that because I'm his mom. Brady and I moved to Texas from Ohio for a job opportunity when Brady was five-years-old. This was a wild adventure on its own, but I had faith that it was the right move for the both of us, so I wasn't that nervous. I discovered that the school district that we moved into had a charter school that offered a dual-language immersion program. How cool is that?! I was shocked at how formal the process was to get accepted into the program; it required an essay from me and an interview with Brady. He was accepted and started his kindergarten year with half of his day immersed in the Spanish language and was in that program for five years. He's now fluent in Spanish and has cultivated tenacity with his love of wanting to learn other languages.

I must have been going by the motto "new state, new me" because our schedule went from doing a little here and there to "let's live." It was probably a mixture of the new job, a little homesickness, and wanting to make sure that we created a solid foundation, but I filled our schedule up. Aside from his school, Brady also started Cub Scouts, soccer, and piano lessons that year. It was a busy schedule and a lot of learning and running around, but it led to us building a wonderful new circle of friends who became family. Seven years later and he's still going strong with Spanish, is learning sign language, is a Boy Scout working towards becoming an Eagle Scout, plays piano and guitar, loves to read, is taking advanced classes, and is a total athlete. You name it, he plays it: football, basketball, baseball, hockey, soccer, fencing, parkour, and weightlifting. While we were in Texas, it was important to me that we didn't lose any connections with our family. I made sure that we didn't miss any holidays or special events, and we tried to see at least his grandparents every couple of months. Thankfully, there were affordable flights between Dallas and Cincinnati, so it made it easy to fly back and forth when we wanted to.

After the breakup with my son's father, I had two relationships that lasted a little over a year each. The first relationship that I was in was full of heartache with multiple miscarriages, and the other just wasn't at the right time. They were both before Brady was five. I was in the mindset that I should have a partner, and that I needed to create this nuclear family life for my son, but what I have learned throughout the years is that every family comes in different shapes and sizes: single-parent households, married households, divorced, and re-married. However your family is structured, it's your life, and if you pour love into it, it's going to be a great one. That's the foundation that I've set for our family: love and hard work. I didn't know what I wanted to do career-wise when I was 20 years old and having my child. I just knew that I wanted to be a mom (and a wife, but that hasn't happened yet). I had this perfect little gift from God and didn't have much else except love and the work ethic to get things done. I knew what kind of life I wanted for us, but wasn't sure how I was going to get there just yet. Once I got away from toxicity and drama, my head started to clear. I started to notice people, how they carried themselves, how they talked, and their choice of words. It was like the fog lifted and everything became clear. When I started surrounding myself with positivity and light, I became positivity and light. Every self-help and mindset book that I could find, I read. I found inspirational women on YouTube giving advice on how to be better and watched them daily. I wanted to do better.

When my income started getting higher, and I wanted to get a grip on my credit, I realized that I couldn't finance a pack of gum if I wanted to. My credit was horrible—400s/500s. At one point I was looped in the payday loan circle—do not do that. I pulled my credit report and started paying things off one by one, and within a couple of years my score went up to the high 700s. You have to visualize what you want and then make a plan for how you're going to get there. Then put your plan into place.

A year into the pandemic, like many others, my son and I were working and schooling from home. Some things were going on with my family in Ohio that I felt we should be home for, so I took the opportunity to move back for a couple of years. I was nervous at first—I think mainly because when we left, I felt as if I had almost escaped, and I worked so hard to create our life in Texas. My therapist advised me to put a goal or limit on how long we would be living in Ohio, so I would give myself time to adjust before reassessing, and I took her up on that. I love the mindset that if we don't like it, we can change it. I wanted to see what it was like to live close to family with a healthy mind, and so far, it's been nice to pop over and see my parents without getting on a plane first.

If you get anything out of this chapter, I want you to understand that you are not alone. You are not stuck. You can do this.

Have faith and make a plan.

Samantha Gregory

CEO of Samantha Gregory Consulting

https://LinkedIn.com/in/samanthagregory
https://facebook.com/mssamanthagregory
https://instagram.com/samanthagregory
https://samanthagregoryconsulting.com
https://RichSingleMomma.com

Samantha Gregory has been empowering women to thrive since 2008 with her blog, books, business consulting, and Blyss LifeTM coaching. She's been featured in The Washington Post, The New York Times, and Essence Magazine.

She is the founder of RichSingleMomma.com™, the first online magazine featuring personal finance, parenting, and personal development for single moms.

She also runs a technology consulting firm that helps tech-challenged entrepreneurs launch and profit faster. Services include tech setup and training. Her clients include: Google, Delta, Verizon, Intuit, and Truist.

Samantha is the author of, No More Crumbs: How to Stop Dating (and Mating) for Crumbs and Get the Cake You Deserve in 10 Crucial Steps!, The Magic Money Formula, and 100 Secrets of Successful Single Motherhood. She has 11 other ebooks and has collaborated on two book projects.

She loves traveling, graphic design, and creating her handmade Blyss Calming Cream.

SAVING SAMANTHA: FINDING HEALING, HOPE, AND HAPPINESS

By Samantha Gregory

For seven days in 2007, I lay curled up in bed crying my eyeballs out and listening to my then-favorite artist's CD. The pain felt like a thousand daggers were piercing my heart, draining the life out of me. I didn't think I would survive the heartbreak. In fact, at times I wanted to die.

"No!!" he said. "I don't want to marry you!"

Those words the love of my life yelled echoed in my ears as the days faded into each other. Eating, bathing, and even breathing were too much energy and effort. I was divorcing my emotionally and verbally abusive husband, quitting my job, and making plans to move out of the house I spent so much time and energy renovating. I was leaving town never to return.

How did my life hit this emotional death spiral? How did it come to this? Didn't he know I loved him and wanted to be with him? I knew my life was a mess after two broken marriages and the string of rebound relationships I jumped into trying to forget him.

How did I get to this point of shameless desperation? Let's rewind...

Foundation of Fear and Self-Hate

I was bullied for most of my childhood by my extended family and classmates. It didn't help that I was awkward and clumsy, which I heard a lot growing up. I was often the target of teasing and name-calling from my grandmother's foster kids because I was quiet, my skin was too dark, or for any number of other reasons. Anytime I cried and complained it incited more teasing and aggravation.

In elementary school, classmates teased and called me names. Pig nose. Big nose. Darkie. And so on. Fortunately, I had two or three friends that

I played with every day who made me feel like I belonged. My parents didn't help me, so I stopped telling them about being bullied.

My self-esteem was being chipped away day by day. I learned to cope and go on with life full of inner rage that I tried to stuff and hide. I continued through school until my parents moved. I was homeschooled and later shuttled off to boarding school. Because I decided it was the only way to get validation, I got good grades and graduated with honors.

Falling Into Victimhood

A couple of years after college I was feeling lonely and aching for love. Living and working in a small town meant attending an even smaller church with no men my age. It was depressing, but I didn't have the courage to leave because my friends were there.

One weekend, a new mystery tall guy (Mr. Tall Guy) came to church and struck up a conversation with me. I asked my dad about him, looking for guidance, but he dismissed me with a vague question about the guy having kids. Nothing else was said, and I didn't ask any more questions.

I decided to date Mr. Tall Guy because he was giving me attention, telling me I was beautiful, and saying, "I love you," when no one else ever did. It was a whirlwind affair complete with exhilarating motorcycle rides, road trips, engagement, amazing sex, guilt trips, repentance, rinse and repeat. Ironically I never met anyone in his family, not even his twin brother or mother. I made him my world and he made me a single mom. I suppose it was the perfect storm for my life; being bullied as a child, being isolated and neglected as a teen, and feeling unimportant and unloved in general.

Before I met him I dreamed of traveling the world and adventure. Even though I was stuck in a small town with no eligible men at my church, I knew I wanted something more. I wanted the freedom to discover the world and live life without fear. I wasn't ready to settle down, but he convinced me that life with him would be filled with travel and the adventure I was seeking.

Dreams Deferred into Single Motherhood

Being a broke baby mama was not the adventure I envisioned. My dream of traveling and exploring the world and then having a thriving business, being married, and having 2.5 kids with my pilot "husbae" was now deferred. Instead of exhilarating travel I got entangled with and impregnated by an unreliable baby daddy who already had three kids.

I ended up working at the county courthouse and living off food stamps, WIC, and Section 8. This was *NOT* how I imagined my life would go.

When I got pregnant with my second child (by another man) I knew I had to get my life together. How could an intelligent woman with a bright future end up being a broke baby mama?!?!

I could not think about that too long, or the depression would deepen its claws into my soul. I mustered up enough determination to turn my life around. I moved to a new city and started building a new life for myself and my children. Little did I know it would be a rollercoaster of success and failure. I worked at a college, so I enrolled to finish my degree in hopes of getting a better job to support my family.

I was juggling work, school, and parenting, but the stress, pressure, and shame were mounting. I was doing the best I could, but I was still feeling lonely and emotionally fragile. Despite all the parts of my life that were going well, I wanted a relationship to help ease the burden I was carrying. **Lesson Learned: Do not, under any circumstances, seek a relationship while you are lonely, emotionally fragile, or to escape your responsibility.**

Marriage #1

After a few dating failures I eventually met a man that I thought was perfect. He was in the singles group I was a member of, he was a deacon in the church, and he always had a smile. We started dating because I thought he was a good Christian man, but I ignored all the red flags because of loneliness and being desperate for love and help. I told him everything about my life and past relationships. **Lesson Learned: Never tell a man you are dating your entire life story or what you are looking for in a man in the first three months of dating. It will backfire.**

On one of our home dates at my house, he took advantage of my kindness and forced himself on me. I was in such a fragile state emotionally that I didn't fully recognize and accept what happened for what it was…date rape. The next day, he piled on the guilt saying "we" shouldn't have done that because "we" were Christians that were supposed to be following God's commandments. I bought into this lie and cover-up because I still wanted to be in a relationship. These incidents kept happening, and I'd feel guilty until I finally agreed to get married after three months so we would not keep "sinning."

The day after we got married the real nightmare began. He immediately became this Dr. Jekyll/ Mr. Hyde character. He was verbally, emotionally, sexually, and financially abusive to me. He was verbally and physically abusive to my kids as well. At church, he pretended everything was perfect with us, but it was a living nightmare.

I finally **snapped out of my emotional fog and fragility** when I saw the bruises on my terrified son's two-year-old body. I went to the police station to file a report, filed a restraining order, then went to my parents. Later, I went to a women's shelter, then a good friend's home for a couple of weeks until I could get my home back and get the locks changed. I divorced him as quickly as I could. With no shared assets or children, it was as simple as filing the paperwork and getting the judge to sign. The marriage lasted for six months.

Over the next few years, **I focused on recovering from my divorce and**

finishing school. I graduated from college with honors and started working full-time as a NASA contractor. I was doing so well that I bought a house and started making small renovations. Pretty soon, I reconnected with and started dating an old school acquaintance. He made himself useful and helped me find someone to do work on my house. After that, he used his connections to help me find and buy a new car after my kids and I were in an accident. We began talking seriously, and he made a lot of future plans and promises that I believed. Eventually, we decided to get married at the courthouse. **Lesson Learned: Never date an old acquaintance or classmate without vetting him like any other stranger. You do not know him.**

Marriage #2

It didn't take long after we got married for me to realize his talk was just talk, and he was not interested in working on the relationship or being a partner/provider. Our marriage was full of unprovoked arguments, trauma responses from my last marriage, and pretense in front of family and friends. He threw the word divorce around like a self-fulfilling prophecy almost every day. I just wanted to raise my kids and have a happy family.

It was too much to bear the daily mental and emotional torment, carrying the financial weight of the marriage, and basically raising a man-child. The straw that broke the camel's back was finding out that he intentionally dated and married me to use me as a sugar mama. I filed for divorce immediately. The marriage lasted two years.

It was 2007 when I had the mental and emotional breakdown that had me begging the love of my life, Mr. Tall Guy, to come rescue me. He had been in the background of every relationship the entire time, acting as a concerned friend and confidant. The embers of hope burned in my heart when my relationships were going sour. When I needed him to truly be there, he refused and crushed my hope and broke my heart.

For 20 years, through two babies, two failed marriages, abuse, bankruptcy, graduating from college, depression, and stress-induced health issues, I still wanted to be with this man. At the end of the day, he did not want me enough to commit to and marry me.

Eventually, I moved back to my home city and started over again. I found a decent job, home, new friends, and tried to normalize life for the kids. I spent time looking deep to find the missing link in my life.

I stayed away from church for a while and focused on prayer, meditation, and study. I needed to find answers to my questions and reevaluate my life and beliefs. I found a new spiritual family and slowly began to mend. As I got to know myself better, I began choosing myself. Being with Mr. Tall Guy or any other man would not make me whole. I had to recognize that what I was searching for was already inside of me.

In 2014, there was a vague attempt to rekindle a relationship with Mr. Tall Guy again. It was clear that it was over, so I initiated a clean heartbreak so the scar would finally heal correctly this time.

Finding Freedom in Self-Love

With the realization that the relationship was dead, I set myself free. I chose myself and my happiness over a fantasy. I could not be fully present in a new relationship until I closed the book of the old one.

Being bullied as a child at home and in school made me vulnerable to abuse as an adult. No amount of overachievement, intelligence, or general common sense could protect me from the deep, unhealed emotional wounds that made me a target of abuse. No self-defense classes, tough exterior, or no-nonsense personality could stand up against the gaping void of loneliness that made me vulnerable to an abuser's manipulation.

The roots of my pain and poor choices were that I felt unloved and invisible, so I became a chronic overachiever and perfectionist. I was hiding my true self: a desperate little girl in need of love and affection. That unloved part of me allowed me to get pregnant twice outside of marriage and attracted toxic men who were abusive to me and my children. All this made me susceptible to the abuse I experienced in my marriages and relationships.

When a girl is not emotionally built up by her dad, she is easily torn down by the wrong man. She will accept crummy behavior because she thinks that is all she is worth. Crumbs.

Until I healed my emotional wounds and stopped hiding my story, I would keep repeating the cycle of abusive family and romantic relationships.

Being a single mom was the scariest thing I've ever done, but it was not a tragedy. It was the catalyst to finding myself and being able to share that it's possible to come out on the other side of this experience a better version of yourself.

Fast forward to the present. My system is clear, my heart is healed, and I've been free from the drug of unrequited love for a long time. I had to go through bankruptcy, health issues, and therapy in the process of healing.

My kids are grown and creating a life of their own. We are still in a constant state of healing, evolution, and self-love. The stigma and shame of single motherhood are no longer a part of me. I'm proud of myself and the courage it took to get through those years.

In the meantime, I have been empowering women to thrive since 2008 with my blog, RichSingleMomma.com™, the first online magazine featuring personal finance, parenting, and personal development for single moms. I also have a business consulting agency, and I coach women at Blyss Life™ women's empowerment coaching. The My Blyssful Life app is currently in development as well. I love creating and selling my handmade Blyss Calming Cream that helps with stress, insomnia, and menopausal symptoms.

I'm the author of, _No More Crumbs: How to Stop Dating (and Mating) for Crumbs and Get the Cake You Deserve in 10 Crucial Steps!_, _The Magic Money Formula, and 100 Secrets of Successful Single Motherhood._

If you are ready to heal your life so you can experience hope and happiness I'd love to coach you through the process. Email me at samantha@samanthagregory.com or visit my website at samantha gregoryconsulting.com/coaching. You can buy my books, courses, and request consulting at samanthagregoryconsulting.com.

Kati Hudson

NASM-Certified Nutrition Coach
Owner, For Your Nutrition, LLC

https://www.linkedin.com/in/katelebrun/
https://www.facebook.com/groups/450294636180275
https://www.instagram.com/katikate802_cnc/
https://www.foryournutrition.com/

Born and raised in Vermont, Kati Hudson enjoys a mix of outdoor activities: hiking, snowshoeing, skiing, and sledding with her two children. Kati works full-time at an ivy league institution while also building her coaching business, For Your Nutrition. She coaches her daughter's soccer team, loves to dabble with crafts, and is an avid reader and loves to learn; her favorite topics are nutrition, biographies, and growth. Reading on the porch, exercising, or spending time with friends near the water are her favorite choices for rest and relaxation.

Kati graduated from Champlain College in 2006 with degrees in sports management and business management; she is also a certified nutrition coach and a youth exercise specialist with a focus on helping others build sustainable healthy habits that fit into their lifestyle. She still resides in Vermont with her two children, her partner, and two dogs (a Newfoundland and a chug).

BLOOM WHERE YOU ARE PLANTED

By Kati Hudson

As the youngest of four raised by parents whose foundation was zero conflict management skills topped with "we stayed together for the kids," I quickly became a master at not making waves. For the most part, I spent my time with my head down and followed the rules. I did the homework, got the grades, and started working at 14. Sports were my outlet; my coping mechanism for keeping the anxiety symptoms I didn't realize I had at bay, and they taught me time management and leadership skills. Three sports, three terms. I started as soon as I could and kept playing straight through to high school graduation. Productivity equaled proof of worth, and if the end product was good enough then just maybe I was good enough, too. Rinse and repeat.

After a failed engagement at the age of 21, I made the decision that I would not have children of my own. Working full-time throughout college left me burned out and confused, and again living with my parents. With all of that, I felt even more devoted to my decision to not have children. Despite the burnout, I enjoyed working; I wanted the flexibility of taking care of just me. I didn't want to worry about who I would let down or make look bad by showing the sensitive person I truly was.

Then, I met a knows-he's-good-looking younger guy who triggered the subconscious "if he likes you, then you must be good enough" need for external validation. He was from a large, close-knit, religious family; a straight-edge wannabe cop. He had a great work ethic, and he said and did all the right things. His potential to grow and be something was strong, and I was excited to grow alongside him in my career. He bought me flowers, protected me, and convinced me that no one else saw me or accepted me like he did.

Our first apartment was so remote there was no high-speed internet access. We played ultimate frisbee, pick-up basketball, had movie dates, hiked, and ran the pool table at a local bar on Saturdays. Due to failed birth control, I got pregnant within the first year. Shockingly, his family was supportive; mine was not. And, just as I was coming to terms with my life changing drastically whether I was ready or not, I lost the baby. I was confused and sad; even then I wasn't allowed to be upset. What was wrong with me? Why did I feel this way? What had I done wrong? At the same time, I was also thinking: don't show emotions; don't make others feel uncomfortable. The outside perspective was that I had no right to be sad because I "had no idea what I was getting into." The questions kept coming: when will you try again? (*What? No.*) When are you getting married? (*Wait, what?*) There was so much pressure.

I still clearly remember standing in the kitchen of our beautiful, internet-less apartment and yelling at each other. "*I don't want to marry you!*" "I don't want to marry you either!" There it was. A sucker punch that took the pressure off while instilling a searing, subconscious fear in me that, at the time, I couldn't quite pinpoint.

We settled in; got comfortable with the status quo. His dream of being a cop had come undone, and with it came a spiral of bad habits and disruptive, costly hobbies. As he grew unhappier and more discontent, the less accepted I became. Each time I gathered up the courage to approach him with my concerns, he'd respond: *"well, I'm unhappy and you don't do enough. I'll be happy when…*

> *"… you start going to therapy."*
> *"… you change your birth control."*
> *"… you start working out."*
> *"… you change; I don't like how you are."*

So I adapted. I altered my behavior and over time stopped showing emotions. It was easier to not make waves.

Over the years, flags waved in various shades of red:

"A customer wanted to get together to play video games. She wanted to thank me for helping her."

"A customer made me cookies because I was so helpful."

"I'm going fishing and I'll be back in 2 hours." Entire days would pass by.

The revolving door of expensive hobbies and bad habits.

I buried myself in work and tried to make a name for myself. When I wasn't working, I was watching sports or perfecting my crafting hobbies. I did try to fit in with his lifestyle. Once, I spent a good portion of a day playing the video game he was addicted to, but I learned nothing and was still confused about the purpose. I really tried to like the things he liked.

Seven years into our relationship, we married and had our first child. I had been promoted at work. He faced losing his job or moving to a city seven hours away from everyone we loved. I was willing to move, but it had to be on agreeable terms. We now had a baby to support, and I enjoyed my work. I was the lead on all things child-related. Nighttime feeding and changing (no sense in both of us being tired, right?); preparing for daycare; dinner, bath, bedtime; scheduling appointments; baby is sick? Stay home. Our outside support system was *here* and I couldn't just move away.

A proposal was made: let's make this move in stages. It was denied. I can still hear his voice on the phone. *"I can't leave my son."*

My heart sank. He wasn't staying for *us*. Another suckerpunch. Let it go, I told myself. I should be happy he's staying for his child.

We continued to maintain our status quo, on the outside at least. We worked hard. After hours, he rested and focused on himself. I tried my best to keep up with all the household tasks, having put the pursuit of my advanced degree on hold when our son was born.

We had a second child; a purposeful decision despite how mean he'd gotten in his disappointment of not moving away. A physically and emotionally painful pregnancy led to a beautiful baby girl that quite literally completed my heart. I was grateful I had forgiven the emotional affair that took place just a few months prior because our family was growing. Deep inside, though, I felt an impending doom. "It's just postpartum emotions," I told myself.

Things became more volatile and emotionally explosive. If he lost a belonging, he was like a bull in a china shop trying to find it while yelling about how messy our life was; that I wasn't doing a good enough job keeping things in place for him. Fights grew fewer and farther between, but when they did erupt, it was safer to ignore my feelings so that I could calm *his* anger. I patiently waited for his potential to return while becoming more and more withdrawn from those I was closest to.

There continued to be little help. He grew angrier and more dependent on finding the right hobby to fulfill him; we grew more distant. I was horribly lonely and hid myself in my duties as a mother and, after the kids were asleep, my cell phone. Telling him how I felt always landed on deaf ears.

In time, I learned that the emotional affair he'd had while I was pregnant with our daughter (because I was "lazy and didn't do anything") was, in fact, a sexual affair. The humiliation of it alienated me even more. I tried to leave, but bringing the kids with me was not an option; he wouldn't allow it. So, I stayed. I worked through my disappointment and heartbreak in silence because I wanted more for my family. However, I told him that if it happened again, we're through.

No one was to know this; I wasn't to share it with anyone, and no one suspected a thing. I continued to work hard and grew through two promotions while slowly losing passion for the hobbies I had before. The day I signed on the dotted line for the biggest promotion to date was the day I learned he was in the midst of yet another affair. Truthfully, I suspected it. But that truth blasted me in the face, and right in front of my mother-in-law. *Still*, I didn't make waves. For *six weeks* I didn't make waves.

One morning, while yelling at my then 4-year-old son, I had a life changing realization. I was yelling at *him* because I was furious with his father. Things escalated with the kids because I had no help from their father. I was tired, touched out, and resentful. He'd hear me at my wits end from the dark and dingy home office and close the door instead of coming to partner in parenting. Those first few years of our children's lives were hands down the hardest of my life. I was judged and blamed for all of the dysfunction. I hated who I was.

It was in that moment on that crisp September morning, yelling at my little boy, that I admitted to myself just how angry I was at my husband.

We separated that night.

There was no fight. No "*what ifs,*" no "*let's take some time and come back to it.*" Instead, it was "*we never should have married. I only proposed because I was forced to by my family.*" Coupled with "*I destroyed you and changed you.*"

It's crazy looking back. All my life I knew exactly how I'd handle situations if I found myself in them.

If I was abused in a relationship, I would leave.

If I was cheated on in a relationship, I'd be gone.

Yet, the reality of life is this: you never truly know *how* you will respond in a given situation until you are face-to-face with it. And when you are, everything you ever thought you knew about yourself will be in question.

I'd been trained well to shield the public from seeing the truth about life behind closed doors. I was understanding when I should have been angry. I was quiet when I should have screamed. Always bending, somehow never breaking. I hoped that maybe someday I would be appreciated for all of the emotional blows and back seats I'd taken. However, each time I realized that recognition would never come, I subconsciously added a brick to the wall I was building. Deep down, I knew each transgression would contribute to the end of this relationship despite my desire to hold on tight and make things work. Sometimes, though, more damage is done if you continue to hold on.

I had to let go. I had to save myself in order to break the cycle of heartbreak and avoid repeating generational trends of "staying together for the kids."

The disappointment I felt for putting up with more than I ever imagined I would was unbearable. I couldn't wallow in it because my kids needed me. Luckily, I had finally gotten sick of my own bullshit. It was time to get back to me. I put my energy into learning, growing, and focusing on me so that I could be better and stronger for *myself* and in turn, for my children.

Despite the heartache that a broken family causes—and in my case, a bit of alopecia—I approached my decision with the same confidence and sense of peace that I did when I first decided I wasn't going to have children. The start of this chapter required me to get real with what needed to happen next: getting organized, creating consistency, washing the walls (literally) of the burden that a harmful marriage left behind, and building a strong foundation around me and my two little ones.

I thrived in my new role, both at work and at home. I felt lighter, freer. It was easier being a single mom of two than being a wife to an absent husband. Yes, it was hard as hell, but it was so much easier at the same time.

I invested in, and continue to invest in, therapy. It was there, after spending the first three years trying to *save* my marriage, that I learned just how abusive and damaging it truly was. There was so much I had not told her because I thought this was normal; at least he wasn't hitting me. He had convinced me, over time, that his behavior was my fault. So I had bent, contorted, and constantly stuffed any negative feelings down to ensure that I didn't detonate the volatility around me.

During the healing process, I read countless books. I was accepted into and attended prestigious professional growth programs. I joined a months-long healthy habit program with strong and successful women who battle anxiety just as I do. I started a network marketing business, which not only taught me better ways of caring for my skin from the inside out, but it also reignited my passion for nutrition and fitness. I studied at 5:00 AM each morning when my kids were home—and practically nonstop when they were at their dad's—to become a certified nutrition coach. Now I have my own business. I've been reunited with relationships I lost in those long years, and I focused on building relationships with strong, determined people who inspire me to do and be more than I ever thought I could. Know this: your tribe *does* matter!

Healing isn't linear. Seeds never sprout the next day. They require gentle cultivation, patience, sunshine, and yes, rain. I have learned more about myself, my wounds, and how to be proud of myself despite them; to accept myself as whole rather than only the bits and pieces that seemed worthy.

That first bloom to appear after you finally plant your feet where you are? It's worth it. Strengthening my roots has created consistency and predictability for my children. My job is to show them how to live a life that's true in every way possible. My responsibility as a mother is to show my kids what a healthy relationship is, and my marriage to their father was not it. The waves of resentment, dysfunction, and emotional violence

I'd spent so much time trying to hide was only providing them with unspoken stress and confusion.

Instead, I choose to live life approaching things that scare me *and* light my fire. I will show them what it means to use their voice and live with heart; to advocate for themselves and for others; and to lead a life worth living in view, not buried in the ground.

Over these last few years, my learning has focused on how nutrition impacts anxiety and mental-wellness. My goal in coaching others is geared toward the *whole person*, alleviating those mental burdens while establishing sustainable habits to help you feel amazing from the inside out. If this resonates with you, email me at kati.hudson.802@gmail.com or find me on IG @katikate802_cnc.

Kyla Biedermann

Author & Navy Veteran

https://www.facebook.com/kyla.biedermann.5/
https://www.linkedin.com/in/kyla-biedermann-402b40189/

Kyla was born and raised in Fredericksburg Texas, leaving in 2012 to Join the United States Navy. She served 8 years as a Cryptologic Technician including one deployment on the USS Nimitz. After becoming a single mother to her son in 2020 she realized the attitudes and culture surrounding single mothers needed to change, starting with her own. This was the beginning of a long journey of self-improvement, self-love, and educating herself in hopes of one day being able to help those facing similar challenges while helping to raise awareness and spread education about single motherhood. She is a full-time mother, employee, and student at a local San Antonio community college where she studies Real estate. Her motto in life is, always learning, always changing, and always growing. In her free time, she enjoys playing video games, swimming, going to museums, shopping, staying active, and staying healthy physically, mentally, and spiritually.

THE PACTS TO SINGLE MOTHERHOOD

By Kyla Biedermann

When I was 19, I experienced a terrible physically and mentally abusive relationship that lasted about nine months. What most people don't understand is that most of these relationships don't start badly, they end up bad, and by the time you realize it's bad you are stuck and almost completely dependent on this individual. Young, vulnerable girls who have not been shown proper love from their families are easy prey for the traps of abusive men and are almost a sure catch in their seemingly harmless traps. Men like this often separate you from your family and friends and they begin to control anything that makes you independent. This is how they control you and eventually mentally, physically, and even sexually abuse vulnerable women and girls. Luckily for me, I was already signed up to go to the United States Navy before this relationship, and that is ultimately what got me away in a relatively quick fashion. Once I was safe and had mentally analyzed the situation, I knew I could never let this happen to me again. I made a pact to myself; I would *never* be in a relationship like this ever again, and if at any point I detected the same red flags or vibes, I would be out of there as fast as I could. I only made one other pact like this to myself before: a pact that I would never get divorced, and I take these pacts very seriously. Family is so important to me, and the reasoning of the pacts was to benefit my future family and give my future children everything I never had.

In January 2012, I joined the Navy. I was very excited about the new start and always remembered my two pacts I made with myself. From that point on I ducked, dodged, dipped, and dove away from even the slightest inkling a man was jealous, controlling, or abusive. For the next eight years, I can't say my dating life was great or that I didn't make other bad choices, but I successfully stayed safe and out of the clutches of abusive men. In 2019 I decided to leave the Navy, and in the months leading up to my discharge, I believed I had finally met the man I was looking for. He was honest, caring, supportive, funny, and made time for me, everything no other man had ever done for me. I was at the lowest of my lows at that point after what I had been through in the Navy, and I was vulnerable. I felt beat down and having someone on my team made everything so much better and bearable. I believed this man was the man of my dreams, and I never once stopped to analyze if there were ever any red flags. Everything was perfect, and I felt like no matter what, life was going to be okay with this man. We were married relatively quickly, but there was no doubt in our minds that we were right for each other.

It was the craziest thing. After we were married, he began to change and do things that ever so slightly brushed against the boundaries of my pact before they grew to become blatant no-goes for me. At first, he was rude to me when he would wake up from a nap because he was grumpy. I brought it up and let him know I was not going to be treated like that, and with his agreeance, it felt like I had drawn a line and put an end to any of that kind of stuff. In the grand scheme of things though, I realized It was just me giving him the benefit of the doubt. The next thing I knew, he was demanding I delete close friends on Facebook and saying that since he was my husband I needed to do what he says. I started to have flashbacks to when I was 19. I coached myself, "Kyla, these are your good friends and there is nothing inappropriate about your friendship with them, and you promised yourself you would never again give up family or friends because of a controlling man." I remembered my pact to myself and refused to let my friends go. I tried to explain how there was nothing wrong with me being these people's friends, and that I could not wait to introduce them in person because he would love all my friends. The next thing I knew, every time I left the house I was being accused of cheating and the most unbelievable things. I had so many conversations with him about how unhealthy this was for our relationship, going to great lengths to prove my innocence, and just trying to get him to think rationally. It never changed anything.

After so many flashbacks to when I was 19, I knew we needed to separate. I hoped he would miss me and remember that he needs to respect and trust me. If he did, we could reconnect. There was no way I was getting divorced though, and I had all the confidence in the world that we could overcome this easily. It was especially hard to come to this conclusion, though, because I had just found out I was six weeks pregnant, but it absolutely could not keep going on like this. After I proposed the separation, he became irate, and for the first time he threatened to physically hurt me, something I had seen coming but refused to believe could happen. It was at that point I was terrified. I released myself from any emotion and did what I trained myself to do for safety and for my future family: separate as fast as possible. That was the last day I ever saw him in person.

That night I cried for both of us. I put myself in his shoes. I knew he was probably never going to see or meet the baby, I knew he was going to miss something really awesome, and I knew he had just lost his family and was on a plane back to his hometown. The reality was immense for both of us. I was now in a mental battle between the pacts I had made to myself so long ago; do I get a divorce and break one pact the save the other, or do I stay with an abusive man to save myself from breaking my divorce pact? These pacts were designed to keep me and my future family safe, and yet now, I had gotten myself into a situation where keeping a pact could danger me or my child. I just could not do it, I could not be with someone that could even utter abusive language toward me, I could not be with someone who was not capable of fostering the loving environment I was working so hard for.

Deciding to get divorced was very hard for me. At the same time, though, I had to come to all the realizations about what was coming with this baby, and I struggled with the thought of being a single mother. First, it was embarrassing to me. I had never seen my life going like this, and I did not want this responsibility. I was terrified about what people would think and say about me, so I kept it off Facebook and dreaded anyone finding out. On top of that, I had never really been around kids, so I knew absolutely nothing about being a mother and now I had this huge responsibility coming that I needed to prepare for. It was the scariest thing ever to me, and I didn't know if I could do it. I was feeling very lost and confused. How do you become a mother? What are you supposed to do? What if I mess something up? How do I know if I'm doing it right? None of these questions have easy answers. I am very analytical, so I like to have a full understanding of what I need to do before I start anything, and I wasn't getting the answers I needed from anyone. One day, I was expressing all of these worries and questions to my stepmother, hoping to learn whatever I could from her and her experience as a mother.

"There is no right or wrong," she explained. "You just do what makes you feel comfortable." At that moment it felt like everything clicked. I was empowered and confident, and I knew what I needed to do. From that moment on, I trusted my maternal instincts and have always done what made me comfortable as a mother. There can be a lot of pressure to act a certain way, buy certain products, or even pressure to perform your motherly "duties" a certain way when you first become a mother. I believe and encourage mothers to focus on doing what makes them comfortable. The more comfortable mom is, the more comfortable baby is going to be, and you can form a much greater bond that way. Learn what your baby likes and dislikes; learn what works and what doesn't with your child. All children are different and require different forms of care and equipment, and focusing on what makes you and your baby most comfortable is what being a mother is all about.

Being a mother has been the most rewarding part of my life, and I am so proud to be a mother and so proud of my son. Since having my son and since announcing on Facebook, I have had such positive feedback from people, and it was nothing like I thought it would be. I learned that all the thoughts I had in my head, were my projections of single mothers, and so I needed to change my thoughts. There is a culture against single motherhood and even motherhood in a lot of aspects that cause people to subconsciously have negative thoughts or feelings about motherhood, especially single motherhood. It can be challenging at times to be a mother regardless of the circumstances surrounding it, and becoming a mother for the first time might be the scariest thing you have ever been challenged with. But this baby is going to be the best part of your life and will show you love beyond anything you have ever experienced. This baby is going to teach you patience and push you to do things you never thought were achievable. Because of my son, I have got my life together. I have learned how to heal and forgive the past, I have learned how to live each day with a purpose, and now I get to tell my story in hopes of helping and encouraging other women who have experienced similar situations. I can truly say that I am a woman after becoming a mother and whether our path includes children or not, isn't that something we would all like to be able to say and believe about ourselves? Becoming a mother is the most beautiful thing that can happen to you, and there are only the most amazing times of your life to look forward to. I am so passionate about encouraging, empowering, and helping others grow, so if my story resonates with you, please feel free to follow and connect with me on my Facebook page, Kyla Biedermann.

Jessica Marshall

President/Owner of American Pools SD

www.americanpoolssd.com

Hey guys my name is Jessica Marshall. I own and operate with my amazing team American Pools Sd in San Diego. I'm a second generation pool builder. My father started his company in 1985 when I was 5 years old. This is where my love for construction and creating beautiful tranquil places for my clients started. I decided to branch off from my family business after 15 years and start my own company. I love it a ton, it's a lot of hard work but I wouldn't change it for the world. I'm a mother of 2 sweet boys 3 & 5. I have an amazing love in my life who has been extremely supportive of me my boys and my career. So very grateful for him.

NEW BEGINNINGS

By Jessica Marshall

A little over a year ago, I became a single mamma of my two beautiful boys, who were ages three and four at the time. This was my second time being a single mom, but I knew that I was capable and embraced the challenge fully. In addition to becoming a single mom for the second time, I was also going through a big transition from taking care of my children and being a home provider, to starting my new business.

When I decided to start my new journey, it was long overdue. I was so beaten down and broken by my relationship. It was time to take back my life and live again. When I walked away from my relationship, I felt like no one would ever want me, because that is what he led me to believe. But the level of toxicity and abuse had reached a new level, and I knew that my boys and I deserved better.

This relationship was difficult to walk away from. Not only were we joined by marriage and the two children we shared, but we also owned a family business together. I knew that walking away meant that I was leaving both our eight-year marriage and the family business I had helped build over the last 15 years.

Coming from an abusive relationship, I know how you can get into a routine of enduring the abuse, no matter how strong of a woman you are. It's not something I enjoy talking about. But, I know there are other women out there going through the same thing, and it is something that happens more than we know. We all need to use our voices to speak openly about it.

When I finally dared to get out of the relationship, life started to look upward for me and my kids. I saw this as an opportunity to reinvent myself in many ways, including taking my health back. My health was also a really important focus for me at the time. I wanted to get back to my pre-baby weight and body, get back in shape, and get my energy back.

I felt like garbage around my ex and his family because they treated me like I was overeating all the time and didn't take care of myself. But what was really happening was that my estrogen levels were so high, they could have killed me. I had put on a total of 100 pounds while in the relationship. I started my weight loss journey by doing a cleanse every month. After the pounds started to drop, I reduced the cleanse to every other month.

People ask, how do you have the energy or time to do this? I started my journey by doing a once-a-month cleanse. This helped restore my energy and helped me achieve my weight loss dream of losing 60 pounds healthily and rapidly. My energy level is through the roof. I feel like I'm 20 again, and I'm 41. I also use a morning supplement that helps keep me balanced and not crave all the carbs and sugars throughout the day.

Of course, I have faced obstacles beyond just my weight loss journey as well. My three-year-old had a severe tongue tie. I arranged for surgery to get it snipped a year ago. I had to learn how to show him unconditional love and keep my patience with him while communicating, without him getting frustrated. It's taken a lot. My son's vocabulary is growing and it has been so exciting to see him push through during the last year. We have had so much one-on-one time, and my boys have bonded. His five-year-old big brother is amazingly compassionate and so loving towards his little brother and his mamma.

As a single mom, it has been important for me to build my own business. One of the things that helped me become one of the fastest-growing pool companies in San Diego in less than a year, is to make sure I have good business relationships with colleagues. I was able to pull together a dream team and make things happen, all while juggling a divorce in the background. Trust was a huge part of my success: making the team trust me and being able to trust them in return. I'm not going to lie, being a woman in construction isn't easy. There were times I wanted to give up, but because of trust, I was able to lean on my support network and keep pushing.

Working in a blue-collar career dominated by men means it's a different kind of world. If you want to be successful, you have to get out there and do the dirty work with your team and give them the respect they deserve. You also have to be strong when men try and take advantage of you. And it doesn't just happen in my industry, it happens in all industries.

When owning a business, I find it very important that when you say you're going to do something, you make sure you follow through. I recommend believing in and standing by your product. You're going to have problems, so fix them and move forward. Communication between yourself and your team is key, even when you don't want it to be. Set proper timelines, and in the end, your team will have a beautiful finished product.

I also recommend branding yourself. Come up with a great name that is something people heavily search for. For example, my colleague suggested my company name: American Pools SD. One, because it's very patriotic, and two, it's the first letter in the alphabet. That means it will appear in organic search engines much quicker.

Through the ups and downs since becoming a single mom and running a business, I have learned how important it is to take care of yourself. I find that when you give yourself your time, it helps fill up your own cup first. Even if it's getting a pedicure, take the time for yourself. I love going boutique shopping and supporting my local woman-owned businesses, getting a favorite meal, or just going to a quiet place. I also love working on my farm with my animals. These are things I enjoy doing during the day or when I get home from work. Ultimately, I always say it's so important to surround yourself with your tribe, from friends, to family, to caregivers, to your children and new love relationships. Doing this really helps to keep your mental health well-balanced with your work life.

I have been so blessed in this new chapter of my life. I own a home and own construction company. I just purchased a tractor for my company, a couple of trucks for the business, and a storage yard for my supplies.

God has also blessed me with the love of my life. He has been very supportive of me in every way. We have been able to balance having my boys and going on dates together. It's so important when you start to date again to make sure you don't feel guilty about spending quality time with your partner. Being happy is the key to being an amazing mom. Being happy also gives you a ton of positive energy.

In life, we all have our spiritual guidance from different religions. I believe in God, but don't ever want to take anyone's religion from them. Pushing through means surrounding myself with the right tribe and not losing my faith in God. That is why I can say I'm able to write this story today.

In life's challenges, here are my words of wisdom. Know you're strong. Know you're loved. Know how important you are. You got this. Push through. There will be moments, there will be days, there will be weeks, and maybe even months when you want to give up. But in the end, when you look back, know that it will get better. You will get healthier, you will get stronger, and you will be the woman that you dreamed of being because you pushed through. Give yourself a high five, eat some chocolate, dance when no one is looking, and enjoy life. Because we only have one opportunity to make it the best life ever. Whatever stage of life you are in, it's never too late to reinvent yourself, so go for it because you are loved.

JOIN THE MOVEMENT!
#SHATTERINGTHESTIGMA

Shattering the Stigma of Single Motherhood
With Dr. Jill Zambon, The Parent Project

The Parent Project was founded in 2022 by Dr. Jillian Zambon, as a way to inspire and motivate single moms. After abruptly finding herself a single mom just weeks before her wedding in 2014, Dr. Jill's focus was instantly on taking care of her daughter and providing her a life that she would have in a two-parent household. She refused to settle for less. Dr. Jill now runs a thriving business that empowers other single moms to come forward and share how they have overcome the obstacles of single parenting to create lives they are proud of– and to help other single moms achieve that, too! She provides conferences for single moms, and women who feel like single moms, to learn about financial independence, how to break generational cycles and trust your intuition again, how to set boundaries, and how to create a more positive mindset. Additionally, she provides staffing placement for single moms and military spouses to put them into more flexible and better paying jobs so they can better balance mom life and work life.

Do YOU want to be an author, and have an inspiring story to share?

The Parent Project offers ongoing authorship opportunities, conferences, and staff placement opportunities. Please visit www.jillzambon.com to learn more about the services and resources available to YOU!

We are always looking for women who want to share their stories of inspiration and become a part of our team of authors!

WHAT WE OFFER YOU

Writing Opportunities

Conferences & Retreats

Staffing Solutions

www.jillzambon.com

Be featured in one of our books, published in 13 countries and sold in all major retailers. Get the visibility you need to LEVEL UP in your business!

Visit www.jillzambon.com to see how YOU can join the #shatteringthestigma movement and be the most empowered single parent you can.

Have you checked out our conferences? Find a conference near you at: https://www.jillzambon.com/opportunities/conferences

Looking to become a sponsor or build a partnership?

Email us at contact@jillzambon.com